MV/SC 3/07

W9-BXG-235

Ferrari 250 GT SWB

Wheels of Dreams

Vintage cars and the people who love them

Text and Photographs
Tom Strongman

Design
Scott Dolash

Kansas City Star Books

Published by Kansas City Star books
1729 Grand Boulevard
Kansas City, Missouri 64108

First Edition, First Printing

Library of Congress Control Number
2006932563

ISBN 1-933466-24-3
Hardcover version

Printed in the United States of America
By Walsworth Publishing Co., Inc.
Marceline, Missouri

Above: Kent Johnson's 1949 Chevy pickup has a perfectly
weathered patina. The chassis and powertrain are from a
late-model truck.

Dust jacket photograph:
Alfa Romeo 8C 2900B Touring Spyder

Contents

Dedication

I dedicate this book to my family, which has shown me the true meaning of the quote from *The Little Prince* by Antoine de Saint-Exupery:

"It is only with the heart that one can see rightly; what is essential is invisible to the eye"; and to my dad, Robert E. Strongman, who gave me my first ride in a sports car and handed me my first camera.

— Tom Strongman

Introduction

Cars are complicated. You cannot explain the appeal of a car simply by its parts or specifications any more than you can describe the character of a person by his eye color or date of birth. To truly appreciate a car, you must know its story, and in the end, a car's story is not about its dimensions, but about its driver.

People are the same. To understand the heart of a person, you need to know his story, and a person's story is not about dates and times, but about the love and passion that steers him trough life. *Wheels of Dreams* is a collection of these stories – stories of vintage cars and the people who love them. But it is more. Through the words and images, another tale is told. *Wheels of Dreams* is my dad's story.

My dad has been a professional automotive writer and photographer for nearly 25 years. Cars and cameras are his passion. But don't get me wrong. My dad's passion has not been defined by his job. Quite the opposite. His job has been defined by his passion. For my dad, this is particularly true when it comes to writing about and photographing vintage cars. To him, cars of yesterday – like a loving grandparent – are a thread woven through the generations, reminding us of what was good and where we came from. My dad has had a lifetime love affair with vintage cars. And to think, it all started with a run-down tamale wagon.

> The frame was jagged and the body battered. The rear hatch had been reconfigured so that hot tamales could be cooked and served street side. To anyone else it was a pile of junk.

It was the mid-1950s, and my dad was in junior high school. His older brother, Jerry, was away in the Navy. The distance and separation were tough, but a letter lit a ray of hope. Jerry promised, when he came home, the two brothers would build a sports car – together. When Jerry returned, he scavenged a beat-up 1949 Crosley station wagon, and as promised, the Strongman brothers reconnected over a car.

The story of the Crosley station wagon begins – fittingly – with another pair of brothers: Powell and Lewis Crosley. At a young age, the Crosley brothers made a $10 bet with their father. The challenge: invent a motor that would drive their wagon. The brothers, of course, won, and from this success stemmed a lifelong ambition to create a viable compact car for the common person.

The Crosley station wagon fit this bill. It was oddly small. The wheelbase was a stingy 80 inches. The tires – 4.5 x 12 – seemed more fitting for a bicycle than a car. The engine was weak but efficient – it got nearly 50 miles to the gallon. The Crosley's round headlights stared from the edges of its distinct bull nose like beady eyes. In contrast to the soft muzzle, the rear was sharp and boxy, capped by a flat, rectangular lift gate. Some Crosley station wagons were polished off with wood paneling or a mustache-like metal grill placed just under its nose.

The Strongmans' Crosley no longer had any such polish. The frame was jagged and the body battered. The rear hatch had been reconfigured so that hot tamales could be cooked and served street side. To anyone else it was a pile of junk. But to the Strongman boys – like the Crosley brothers before them – the station wagon was a lump of clay ready to be molded into a gem.

They tore off the scarred body, leaving nothing but a skeleton. The new body, a Model A Ford Coupe, was found lying in an Illinois farm field. It took only a few bucks to acquire. The bigger Model A had to be reworked and resculpted to fit the smallish Crosley skeleton. In contrast to the Crosley body, the Model A shape was easy on the eyes – it had a bit more flair and a bit less utility. The wheels were open, and with hotrod tires, they looked like a panther's paws hanging off of the narrow body.

A 1939 Ford flathead V-8 formed the soul of the vehicle. The V-8 kicked with 85 horsepower, in stark contrast to the puny 26 horsepower of the original Crosley engine. To an outsider, it must have looked awkward. But to my dad and his brother, the miniature hot rod was as cool as any car in town.

Somewhere in the years that followed, the Crosley hot rod was passed on. The brothers moved on as well – to different cities, different careers, different lives. But to this day, it is cars that unite the Strongman brothers. A car race or show will draw them back together – allowing them time to catch up and time to once again reconnect. And at the root of this brotherly bond, there will always be the memory of a beat-up

Tom and his older brother Jerry started to build a sports car, but this crusty Crosley became the basis for a hot rod with a flathead V-8 and a Model A body instead.

tamale wagon.

My dad has owned a lot of cars in the years since that Crosley hot rod. Some of them have been interesting – he had a bright orange Ford Fiesta that looked more like a pumpkin than a car – but he has never owned another vintage car. That is where *Wheels of Dreams* comes in.

A few years ago, my dad began featuring vintage cars in his column in *The Kansas City Star*. As it turned out, this unlocked something in him. He was reinvigorated. Now he was able to use his camera to create works of art and his pen to tell the untold stories of people and how cars have touched their lives. My dad invests a part of him-self in each classic car he features, just as an artist puts a bit of himself in each painting. Now, thanks to those that have so graciously shared their cars with him and the paper's readers, he owns a small piece of many vintage cars. In that way, *Wheels of Dreams* is really my dad's dream come true.

— Jon A. Strongman

Dreams of Passion

Chapter One

My dad was a Buick man. The first family car I remember was a dark-green 1950 Buick Special two-door fastback, and my dad quickly dubbed it the Green Hornet. He loved the straight-eight engine and Dynaflow transmission.

We lived in Decatur, Ill., and my dad had just started working as a photographer for the newspaper. When he was at work my mom wheeled that Buick as if she were delivering a load of moonshine. Hunched over the wheel, elbow out the window, she mashed the gas like she was trying to stamp out a cigarette butt. A trip to the country was a roller-coaster ride. I'll never forget one particularly memorable ride. Mom pulled out to pass a slow-moving farmer's truck on a two-lane blacktop doing at least 50 miles per hour. As we began to pull alongside, the farmer started a left turn in front of us. Mom hit the brakes, cranked the wheel and spun the Green Hornet into the ditch. Gravel spraying against the bottom of the car sounded like a machine gun. I bounced around the back seat so hard I wondered whether we were upright. The farmer pulled us out of the ditch with his tractor.

Dad's second Buick was a 1955 Century. He proudly called it "a four-holer" because it had four of Buick's trademark portholes in each front fender. Four portholes meant the engine was the 322-cubic-inch V-8 from the Roadmaster. The Century had a small body and a big engine, and it was fast. My dad gunned the red, black and tan hardtop all over town, but he liked to loosen its reins when he drove to his fishing club's cabin in the country. More than once he bragged about pegging the speedometer on the way back to town.

Dad's last two Buicks, four-door Roadmasters, were his glory. They were the kind of car he had only dreamed of owning as a young man. His first was a 1992. When Buick announced the Roadmaster would be discontinued, he traded his '92 for a '96 so he could have one last grasp at Buick's brass ring.

The rear-wheel-drive Roadmasters were very similar to the Cadillac Fleetwood, and that always tickled dad. His '96 had a 260-horse-power V-8, and I always shuddered at the thought of an 80-year-old man leadfooting his way through traffic.

For a reason he never explained, my dad always backed into his uphill driveway. I figured it was an ingrained habit born of his career as a newspaper photographer. For most of his adult life he was on alert in case an editor called him to shoot the latest catastrophe or accident, and even in retirement, when he knew those calls would come no longer, his car always pointed down the drive, ready to go on a moment's notice.

Backing up his driveway was not always without incident. He often scraped the side on the garage door trim. His usual trick was to nose into the driveway across the street, slam the gear lever into reverse and zoom backward up his drive in a straight shot. One day, however, he performed this maneuver without looking for passing cars. He backed into the car of a passing neighbor. "He knows I always back across the street," my dad said indignantly. Fortunately, the damage was minor.

I drove dad's Buick to the hospital during the last days of his struggle with cancer. His presence inside the car was vivid and reassuring. His car was dotted with reminders of who he was: the press-photographer's decal, his Elks lodge medallion, the garage-door scrapes along the side. And stuck to the dash was a tiny magnet that said: "If I can't take it with me, I'm not going."

— by Tom Strongman

'31 Studebaker Speedway

Robert S. Armacost sold Studebakers 50 years ago
Grandsons Don and David now collect them

S tudebaker blood runs deep in the Armacost family.

Robert S. Armacost owned a Studebaker dealership in Indianapolis in 1926. In 1930 he moved to Kansas City and opened a Studebaker dealership. He was president of the National Automobile Dealers Association in 1953. In 1956 he began selling Pontiacs. He ceased business in 1967.

Today, his grandsons Don and David are avid admirers of cars in general and Studebakers in particular. They are surrounded by dozens of Studebakers and other memorabilia that are owned by their company, Peterson Manufacturing in Grandview.

Peterson also has a small restoration company, Studebaker Specialists, whose four employees, Brian Neher, John McCall, Brian Veal and Christopher Mather, maintain and restore the company's collection.

When Armacost's company bought a 1931 Studebaker President roadster in 1999, he turned

Don Armacost's car collection, and specifically his Studebakers, is a reflection of his automotive passion.

the guys loose. They restored it as a replica of the Speedway model, and their work is exemplary. The long, powerful roadster has an amazing presence, and the restoration is startling in its quality.

Every tiny detail, down to the stainless steel spoke covers on the Budd wire wheels, is accurate. The black paint is flawless and the chrome is as smooth as glass. McCall made a top, upholstered the seats and even fabricated molds so he could cast new rubber mats.

"This restoration is their best one to date," Armacost said.

If Robert Armacost had a Studebaker gene, he certainly passed it on to his grandsons. ∎

John McCall's handiwork is most evident in the interior of Armacost's roadster. He upholstered the seat, made the top and molded new rubber floor mats. Speedway roadsters were available in black or gray with red trim.

The High Compression Speedster

The Speedway was a hotter model of the President roadster. It had a high-compression cylinder head, larger carburetor jets, a high-lift cam and a 3.47:1 rear axle ratio. The sleek two-seater was available in Chessylite gray or black. The chassis, wheels, cylinder head and the bottoms of the fenders were painted bright red. The seat was upholstered in red leather. The American Automobile Association required record holders to be production vehicles, so 100 Speedways were built.

In 1931, George Hunt, a Studebaker research engineer, drove a Speedway roadster to eleven speed records at Dry Lake in California. It covered 100 miles at an average speed of 90.35 miles per hour.

'57 Chevrolet Bel Air

Frank Thompson has always been a Chevy fan

Frank Thompson has a fondness for all Chevrolets, and he has an impressive collection of them. In addition to absolutely pristine models from 1952, 1955, 1956, 1957 and 1958, he still has his dad's completely original 1951 four-door. He also has a 1938 Chevy and a couple of Model A Fords.

Thompson, a Jeep dealer in Overland Park, Kan., drove Chevys as a teenager, and one of his first jobs in the automotive business was in the parts department of a Chevrolet dealer. He later worked for a Pontiac dealer who taught him all phases of the business. He bought his first dealer-

Frank Thompson drove Chevys as a teenager, and now he has a fine collection that includes some of the most desirable models.
His all-original '57 Bel Air is close to perfection.

Thompson's collection includes pedal cars, automotive signs and numerous other automotive items. His cars are as spotless as the floor on which they sit.

ship in 1981.

Thompson is a perfectionist, and the vehicles in his collection are stunning.

Four people at his dealership restore his cars to like-new condition, and their restorations are works of art.

He found his 1955 Bel Air through a friend at his church, and he has owned his 1952 Chevy twice. He sold it but bought it back at the invitation of the buyer's wife when the man died. Thompson and his crew refurbished the engine compartment, and it looks brand-new.

It's hard to single out one car from Thompson's collection, but his bright red '57 Bel Air hardtop is incredible. He found it in Texas. Every detail is perfect, just like the day it rolled from the assembly line. The 270-horse, 327-cubic-inch V-8 has two four-barrel carburetors.

Thompson also collects pedal cars and memorabilia, such as signs, models, gas pump globes and even a Whizzer motorbike.

Cars have been Thompson's business for years, but he has loved cars since he was a youngster. His collection is a reflection of that love. ∎

’46 Jeep

Restored Jeep becomes a gift of renewal

Barbara Clouse, center, was surprised when her husband, Randy, and daughter, Mindy Gore, restored her Jeep as a Christmas present when she battled cancer.

C hristmas Eve is a time of sharing and anticipation, but Barbara Clouse was completely unprepared for the surprise her family had in store for her.

Clouse, of Lexington, Mo., was engaged in a battle with cancer that included two surgeries and chemotherapy. Her family thought she needed a distraction, not to mention encouragement, so her husband, Randy, son Adam, daughter Mindy Gore and son-in-law Shane Gore hatched a surreptitious plan to restore her 1946 Jeep as a surprise.

Barbara has loved the little Jeep since her late father, Bobby Wallace, bought it in 1970. She has fond memories of piling into it with her brothers as her dad wheeled them around Lexington. He was always so proud of it. The engine, he always said, "ran like a sewing machine."

Barbara's dad eventually gave her the Jeep, and as a young mom she treated her kids to rides like the ones her dad gave her. As her kids began to drive, they, too, bounced the old Jeep through farm fields.

Barbara hoped to restore the Jeep one day, but that plan slipped to the back burner once she was engaged in her battle with cancer.

Her family, however, decided the restoration would be a good Christmas present.

Randy Clouse owns the service station in Dover, and he slipped the Jeep into the garage behind his station. Along with Adam, Mindy and Shane, Randy stripped the car, removed the body, and painstakingly began bringing Barbara's Jeep back to like-new condition.

Barbara often wondered why her husband was spending so many extra hours at his shop.

On Christmas Eve of 2005, the Clouse family parked the finished Jeep in Mindy's garage. By feigning a foot injury, Mindy got her mom to leave her Christmas dinner preparations and come to her house.

Instead of an injured daughter, Barbara found her bright red Jeep sitting in the garage with a big red bow. Once she regained her composure, she fired up the engine. It still "ran like a sewing machine."

Barbara's cancer is gone, and she and her Jeep have been renewed. ■

Clouse grew up riding around in this Jeep with her dad, Bobby Wallace, and her brothers. Her family now rides in it, especially since it has been restored to such fine condition. Her Jeep holds more than 30 years of memories that revolve around her family.

'27 Packard

Wilbur Haupt hits the road in his restored Packard

Wilbur Haupt and his 1927 Packard have been buddies for more than 50 years. They've traveled thousands of miles together, and they know each other well.

This Rollston-bodied Packard is a car of amazing presence and considerable merit. All of the bright work is nickel, not chrome, and the detailing is exquisite. The door handles alone are works of art.

The long-stroke, eight-cylinder engine is smooth and strong. The 143-inch wheelbase is as long as a double-cab pickup. The back seat has as much legroom as a dance hall.

Haupt, of Overland Park, Kan., grips the gigantic wooden steering wheel with a delicate touch, and he steers gently, as if he were guiding an old friend. His fingers slip to the wheel's hub to adjust

the spark advance with such practiced precision that he doesn't even take his eyes from the road.

He changes gears deftly, feeling when it's just right to move to the next gear with nary a crunch from the unsynchronized transmission.

Haupt lived in Pennsylvania when he discovered this rare Rollston-bodied treasure in a barn in upstate New York. Rollston was a coach builder that made bodies to order much like a tailor makes a suit.

The Packard had been ignored for years. The paint was weathered, chains were on the wheels, and mud was everywhere. The owner had used it like a truck. The engine ran but had some piston slap. Haupt drove it home, but he had two flat tires because the front end was bent.

In spite of the car's rough condition, Haupt and his family enjoyed their Packard for years. He started its restoration not long after he retired in 1989. The body went to one shop and the engine to another. The car was so sound, he didn't even take the body off the frame.

Haupt, who has an engineering degree, has a fine feel for detail. To get the wheels pinstriped accurately, he built a wooden platform with Lazy Susan bearings. The striper could touch his brush and spin the wheel to make perfectly concentric circles.

The full restoration took about three years, but working out all the bugs so the car was reliable on

When Haupt found his Packard in upstate New York, it was being used as a truck. Haupt restored it to exceptional condition. It is so reliable that he drives it on long trips, including one to Ohio in 1999. Haupt rarely misses a chance to slip behind the wheel for a spin.

the road took an additional year. Haupt added an electric fuel pump and auxiliary turn signals to make his car more roadworthy.

In spite of its rarity, Haupt's Packard is not a trailer queen. He gets behind the wheel whenever he has a chance, and he thinks nothing of driving it a couple of hundred miles. He has driven it more than 8,000 miles since its restoration. The longest trip was more than 2,000 miles, when he drove to Warren, Ohio, for the Packard centennial in 1999.

"It was built to be driven," he said, "and I really like driving it." ∎

'50 Dodge Wayfarer

Joe Egle likes cars that are a part of his history

Cars are as much a part of Joe Egle as his DNA. This one-time imported-car dealer has tinkered with and collected cars most of his adult life. It's clear from his conversations that cars are connected to significant events in his life. He owns an Austin-Healey Sprite that was built the same month his daughter was born, and his 1950 Dodge Wayfarer Sportabout is one of his favorites.

A framed magazine article about Egle hangs on the wall of his house with the following quote: "Cars are my obsession. When I was in the service and left behind my 1950 Dodge roadster, I missed that more than anything."

Egle is one of Kansas City's automotive raconteurs. His house is plastered with photographs, license plates and models of cars he has owned and loved.

Before being shipped overseas, Egle served in the Air Force at the Pentagon in 1954. He bought a 1950 Dodge roadster from a widow for about $550. The Wayfarer Sportabout was different from other Dodge convertibles because it was a three-passenger. It had no back seat. It sold new for $1,727, making it, Egle said, one of the cheapest convertibles in 1950. It was discontinued in 1951.

The Wayfarer Sportabout, about 6 inches shorter than a regular Dodge, was built on a shortened 115-inch wheelbase. Because it had no back seat, the trunk was cavernous. A coupe and a two-door sedan were also built. Power comes from a 103-horsepower, 230-cubic-inch six-cylinder that uses fluid drive, a semi-automatic transmission in which a fluid coupling replaces the flywheel, allowing shiftless driving.

Simplicity is one

The Dodge Wayfarer was an unusual sight in 1950 because it did not have a back seat.

reason Egle likes his Dodge. In 1954, while driving it to Kansas City from Virginia, he encountered tornadic winds near St. Charles, Mo., and the original top was blown off. After he arrived in Kansas City, he had a new top installed for $35 while he took a long lunch.

Egle sold his Dodge Wayfarer Sportabout in 1956 but bought another nearly 20 years ago. He has owned and raced numerous vintage cars, including a Jaguar C-Type, but he still likes his Dodge. It is, he said, one of the only cars he has ever dreamed about.

Cars and dreams often go together. For Egle, whose life has been centered around automobiles, giving life to his dream is as simple as sliding behind the wheel of his Dodge Wayfarer Sportabout and turning the key. ∎

'39 Ford Deluxe

Joe Egle's 1939 Ford Deluxe coupe is a pristine example of why Henry Ford's products were so widely admired. The streamlined body is exquisite in its simplicity. It looks fast just sitting still. The headlights have glass covers whose shape perfectly mirrors the curvature of the fender.

The 221-cubic-inch flathead V-8 cranked out 85 horsepower, enough to give the lightweight coupe sparkling performance.

Egle bought this coupe a couple of years ago in North Carolina, and he had a nifty back seat installed, converting it to an "opera coupe."

"I have two granddaughters who need to have seatbelts," Egle said, "so I had LeBaron Bonney install the back seat." LeBaron Bonney, of Amesbury, Mass., specializes in interiors, tops and carpets for Ford cars from 1928 to 1954.

Egle said his black Ford "is the sweetest driving car" he owns.

Egle added a back seat to his Ford coupe so his granddaughters would have a place to ride.

'38 MG TA Tickford

Sandy Krug's near-perfect example of a rare MG.

Sandy Krug's 1938 MG TA Tickford Drophead Coupe is as spotless as the day it rolled out of the factory. Maybe more so.

Tickford is the name of the custom coachwork built by Salmon and Sons of Newport Pagnell, Buckinghamshire, England. The company began building horse-drawn carriages but switched to building custom bodies for automobiles. Slightly more than 300 Tickfords were built, and Krug speculates that only 35 or so are in this country.

After the MG TA chassis, firewall and fenders were completed at the factory in Abingdon, the car was driven down the road to Salmon and Sons, where craftsmen installed the custom Tickford body, interior and top. Tickford patented its three-position folding top, which the English call a drophead. The drophead could be closed, partly open or completely open. Along with the clever top, roll-up windows and a fixed windshield gave the Tickford the protection of a closed car and the freedom of an open one.

The TA has a 1,292-cc, four-cylinder engine that produces about 50 horsepower. It cost more than twice as much as a Chevy when new.

Sandy and Barbara Krug's MG has won numerous trophies for its near-perfect restoration. The MG does more than just collect trophies, however. On sunny afternoons, the Krugs are often found behind the wheel.

Krug's fascination with MGs began in 1974, when he saw one for sale on the street. He stopped, bargained with the owner and bought it on the spot. Krug, of Prairie Village, Kan., drove it home.

By 1984 he really had the bug. When his wife saw an ad for a

TA for sale in California that year, Krug called and said: "Please don't sell the car until I can get there this weekend." He flew out on Friday night, bought the car on Saturday and flew home Sunday. It was, he said, an expensive weekend.

He began restoring it in 1995. Craig Vaughan of Foreign Car Enterprise of Kansas City did the mechanical and electrical work. Jeff Deutch of JMD Restorations in Platte City did the body, and Joe Poindexter of Ace Auto Fabric of Kansas City reupholstered the interior working from old photographs.

Krug has shown his MG all over the country, and his family room is full of trophies. It has appeared at the prestigious Meadow Brook Concours d'Elegance in Detroit and the Pebble Beach Concours d'Elegance in California.

Tickford patented the three-position folding top that gave the MG the protection of a closed car with the freedom of an open one.

'69 Camaro

Kevin Phipps tracks down his first car

Kevin Phipps said that getting his hands on this 1969 Camaro — the second time — was like hitting the lottery.

Phipps, of Excelsior Springs, Mo., first bought this car in 1977. It had big wheels and a hot V-8. He was young, and it was fast. He drove it to college in Warrensburg, Mo., where he met Debbie, now his wife. Because the Camaro was expensive to drive back and forth to school, he sold it after a couple of years. That was late 1979.

Skip ahead about 20 years. When Phipps began to think about restoring an old a car, his wife, Debbie, quipped: "What if you could find your old Camaro?" The search was on, but finding it would be nearly impossible because he had only a license number. Missouri's Department of Revenue does not have computerized records for 1979, and requests to track down old VIN numbers can take months because folders have to be thumbed individually. Phipps hired a private investigator to track the vehicle's history, but the trail went cold after he found that the car was sold to an unkown person in St. Joseph. Phipps thought it was hopeless.

Then one Saturday, Chris Blakley, a friend, asked how the search was going. When Phipps explained the Camaro's trail was last known to be in St. Joe, his friend said he had an acquaintance who mentioned that he saw an orange Camaro sitting in the back of a St. Joe body shop. Phipps phoned the shop and then went to visit. Sure enough, the VIN number matched. It was his old car. The windshield scratch was still there, and the dash pad screwed down by Phipps and his dad was still intact. Even the cracked rear panel hadn't been replaced.

Kevin Phipps thought his first car was lost for good, but a friend found it sitting in the back of a garage. Today it looks like new again.

Phipps bought the car, although he chuckled and said that he paid more for it than he got when he sold it.

He towed the Camaro back to Excelsior Springs. He ripped out the interior and repaired rusted floorboards. He took the car to Quality Body Works in Lawson, Mo., where Gary Van Hooser replaced most of the body panels. Lloyd Johnson of Accent Auto Trim re-upholstered the interior. Justin and Bill Skinner, friends of Phipps, helped take the engine out and put it back.

In a little over a year, the orange Camaro looked better than new. Today, the exhaust pipes rumble like a cat purrs. Phipps was rewarded with a tro-phy in his first car show.

Phipps and his Camaro seem to have some mysterious karma. While his perseverance was a factor in locating the car, it took more than a little luck to actually find it. Now it sits back in his garage, in like-new condition. ∎

'49 Studebaker Champion

This tan sedan courses through the Beyer family

Four generations of Beyer boys have wielded the keys to this Studebaker sedan. Kent, left, his dad, Rick, center, and his uncle, Brad, are but a few who grew up driving this car.

When Arthur F. Beyer bought his Studebaker Champion for $2,097.55 on March 11, 1949, there was no way he could predict the effect his car would have on his family for the next 57 years. Like the current of the Big Blackfoot River in Norman Maclean's *A River Runs Through It*, this modest four-door sedan has coursed through his family with a steady rhythm: father to son, father to son.

Four generations of Beyer boys have wielded the keys to this tan four-door with its racy red wheels. The list of drivers reads like a biblical genealogy. Every time a son, a grandson or a great-grandson grips the thin plastic wheel of this family heirloom, Arthur Beyer's spirit is sure to be alongside.

Arthur Beyer died in 1952 at age 56. Beyer's wife, Emma, drove the car just 6,000 miles in the 16 years after his death. The canceled check, the bill of sale and Beyer's handwritten journal describing trips are like new.

The car's remarkable procession through the family began in 1968 when Art Beyer moved it from Cleveland to Texas. His son Brad, who now lives in Shawnee, drove it during his sophomore, junior and senior years. "We didn't have concerns about salt roads, so I drove it year-round," Brad said. "Then my brother drove it during his high school years. When he graduated in 1976 it was parked for a while and began a general deterioration. My dad, already thinking about grandchildren even though none were in sight, gave it to a high-school shop class in 1985 and asked them to fix it up.

"My dad was real proud because by the time my son Brandon was ready to drive in 1994, we went to Texas and hauled it up here on a trailer. Brandon immediately drove it over to a girlfriend's house, and it spewed steam all over because it had the wrong radiator cap. We were in the shop pretty regularly. Brandon had mixed feelings about driving the car. He wanted a car that was a little sexier, a little speedier, a little more muscular — something sleek and fast. I liked it because it was kind of big, kind of slow and very recognizable. The police in Shawnee knew it belonged to that Beyer kid, and he couldn't get away with anything."

The stories this car could tell. From Arthur and Emma Beyer's cross-country trips in the 1950s to teen-agers learning to drive a stick shift in the Shawnee Mission Northwest parking lot. ("The yellow lines were cars, and we hit 39 the first time," Brad said.)

About 1997, Brandon went to college. That's when the car was transferred to Brad's cousin and current owner, Rick Beyer of Leawood. "Loyalty in this family," said Sarah Beyer, Rick's wife, "runs wide and deep."

"I didn't really want it at first," Rick said, "but Erik fell in love with it and got me interested in it again. He drove it to school. We decided to carry on the tradition that Brad started. We took it to

Precision Restoration in Independence, and Jim Barber took it apart and put it back together in the pristine condition it is now. Two of the hubcaps came from Australia."

The Beyer's Studebaker has been a constant through generations of change. Family members today steer the same wheel that Arthur Beyer did when he first drove home from Koepke Motors that March in Cleveland. Like Maclean said in his book, traditions restore the soul and stir the imagination.

Even today, Rick said, "when I take the wheel I can almost imagine grandpa and what he felt like." ■

'63 Mercury

Ben Green drove his first 427 when he was in high school

Ben Green has been interested in big-block Mercurys since he was in high school. Kennith Johnson bought this car for $4,096 in 1963. That year, Mercury built only 58 cars with the 425-horsepower engine.

Ben Green of Chillicothe, Mo., has been fascinated with the 427-cubic-inch Mercury since he drove Dr. Oliver Duffy's Park Lane in 1964.

Green lived in Trenton, Mo., at the time, and during high school he ran errands for Helmandollar Lincoln-Mercury.

"Doc lived north of Trenton. He never brought his car in for service," Green said, "so I would go get it." Doc's 427 carved such an image in Green's memory that for years he tried to track one down.

Locating one was difficult because only 58 Mercurys with the 425-horsepower, 427-cubic-inch V-8 and two four-barrel carburetors were built in 1963. Forty-two were built in 1964

and eight in 1965. By comparison, Ford produced 5,389 Ford Galaxies with the 427 engine in 1963 alone.

These big-engined Mercurys had quite a racing history. The fastback roofline contributed to high-speed performance. Parnelli Jones won the Pikes Peak Hill Climb with one in 1963 and 1964. Jones also wheeled a 427 Mercury to the Late Model Championship of the United States Auto Club in 1964.

An acquaintance found this car and sold it to Green. According to the original invoice, which Green has, Kennith Johnson originally purchased Green's car on June 11, 1963, in Gadsden, Ala., for $4,096. He traded in a 1950 Chevrolet. It's an interesting coincidence that Green's parents lived in Gadsden in the 1970s and 1980s before moving to Trenton.

Green's Peacock Turquoise Mercury has 76,000 miles. The bumpers have been rechromed and the seats recovered with NOS seat material, but the car is remarkably well- preserved.

"You normally wouldn't think of a Mercury as a fast car," Green said, "and I probably wouldn't have wanted one if I hadn't driven Doc's. It's neat to own a piece of automotive history." ∎

'28 Studebaker President

August Grasis fulfills a childhood promise

August and Ruta Grasis left Latvia in 1944. He got an engineering degree in Germany and came to the United States in 1950. His 1928 Studebaker is nearly identical to the one taken from his family by Russian soldiers in 1940.

In 1940, with tears in his eyes, August Grasis watched as Russian soldiers towed his father's 1928 Studebaker President away from the family home in Riga, Latvia. This teenage boy promised himself that someday he would get his parent's car back.

The Grasis' family's businesses and apartment building were confiscated during the Russian, and then German, occupation of Latvia. "That was the worst time in my life," Grasis said.

More than six decades later, August Grasis again has a 1928 Studebaker President. It's not the car that was towed away, but it is one he has restored as closely as possible to the one of his youth. This polite and genteel man made good on his promise to himself.

Grasis has always been fascinated with cars. As a young boy in Latvia, he spent most of his spare time in the garage with the family driver, Karl Skulte. Mr. Skulte, as Grasis always calls him, was almost like a member of the family. Once, when Grasis' mother left her passport behind after boarding a train for Berlin, Mr. Skulte, with Grasis at his side, raced the Studebaker to the

border, beating the train. "We caught it," Grasis beamed. His mother got her passport.

Mr. Skulte taught Grasis to drive. Once, on a winter trip to the country, Mr. Skulte had Grasis, about age 13, take the wheel. With the whole family aboard, Grasis, eager to demonstrate his prowess, banged a fender into a tree when he hit a snow drift.

In 1944, Grasis and his wife, Ruta, left Latvia on a ship for Germany just before the Soviets reoccupied the country. He got a civil engineering degree in Stuttgart, Germany. The couple came to the United States in 1950 as displaced persons and lived in Chicago before moving to

Grasis replicated the colors of his family's car when he restored this one. He always puts fresh flowers in the Studebaker's back-seat bud vases when he takes the car for a drive. A beautiful trunk is fitted to the luggage rack.

Kansas City in 1965. Grasis became a successful businessman, and he now maintains a foundation that helps support pensioners in his native Latvia.

In 1990, Grasis saw a Studebaker President at a vintage car event in Colorado and realized it was time to pursue his childhood promise. He joined the Studebaker club and searched the globe for a 1928 seven-passenger President. There were four. He bought one in Boston and gave it complete restoration. It is as much like the one his family used to own as he could make it.

As I met Grasis at his garage to go for a drive, I

found him cutting fresh flowers. Placing a handful of yellow flowers into each crystal vase, he said: "I never drive it without fresh flowers."

When Grasis settles behind the wheel of his Studebaker President, his hands fall lightly onto the steering wheel with a familiarity remembered from childhood. Each gear shift is like shaking hands with an old friend. As we motor serenely in his elegant auto, his gentle smile mirrors memories of his youth. Like the fresh flowers in his car, his youthful promise to someday have another Studebaker blooms anew. ■

'33 Studebaker Indy racer

August Grasis and his son Augie have a deep love for automobiles. Their garage holds examples of vintage cars that have meaningful spots in their lives, but their 1933 Studebaker Indy racer touches their heart in a special way.

Grasis' car was one of a team of five Studebaker racers entered in the Indianapolis 500 by the factory in 1933. It is the only one left that still wears the high-cowl, aerodynamically efficient bodywork that was developed in the University of Michigan wind tunnel.

Augie and his dad race their Studebaker regularly. They have driven it in vintage Indy car events at the Milwaukee Mile and lapped the Indianapolis Motor Speedway along with other vintage racers. Augie often drives it in vintage sports car races.

When its straight-eight engine gets wound up, it sends shivers up your spine like a spring thunderstorm.

It is only fitting that No. 34 now resides in Kansas City, because its driver in the 1933 Indianapolis 500 was Tony Gulotta from Kansas City. Gulotta qualified at 113.678 mph and finished in seventh place.

Old race cars are meant to race, and they are never more alive than when they are pounding around a track. The Grasis family has given No. 34 a new lease on life. Tony Gulotta would be proud. ∎

Dreams of Love

Chapter Two

The hot August sun scorched Interstate 70 as my future wife, Susan, and I droned across the eastern plains of Colorado, Missouri-bound. This was our first car trip together. Days earlier, we had decided to get engaged and I quit my summer job with the Colorado Department of Transportation. We were headed east in my very first car, a dark blue 1958 Volvo 444. The sky was vast and the landscape as sparse as my plans for the future. But I had my car, and I had my girl.

That was 1966, just months after I had graduated from the University of Missouri. I had spent the summer in Denver with my brother's family. My boring job with the highway department consisted of riding in a pickup with a clipboard on my lap, cataloging every sign and signal on every inch of the state highways that went through Denver and its suburbs. My driver and I moved like an inchworm. The job was bureaucratic busywork created in response to the enactment of the Highway Beautification Act, a pet project of Lady Bird Johnson.

My wife-to-be came to Denver to visit for a few days, and while there we decided to start wedding plans. I called my boss, quit over the phone and loaded the Volvo for the trip to Missouri.

The Volvo was as dear to my heart as only first cars can be. It looked like a miniature 1948 Ford. The 444 was the first Volvo imported to this country in 1958, and its 1.6-liter engine had a meager 85 horsepower in spite of the fact that it had two carburetors. My car's engine felt as if some of its 85 horses had already been put out to pasture. The first time I mashed the throttle for a run through the gears, the throttle linkage stuck wide open and only a quick flick of the key kept me from running off the road or ruining the engine. I never floored the throttle again without remembering that day.

Because the Volvo was my first car, I had a lot of first-car urges to get out of my system. Off came the bumpers for a sleeker look, and on went big wheels, created by welding Volvo wheel centers into wide Buick rims. I mounted the biggest tires that would fit under the fenders. I wrapped the steering wheel with twine, like sports car racers from the 1930s.

With its hopped-up stance, my little Volvo looked pretty tough, even if the engine was rather anemic. What it needed was a little more bark, even if there wasn't much bite. I replaced the original muffler with a glass-packed one. I angled the exhaust pipe so it exited under the passenger's door, like a stock car. I welded on an old chrome motorcycle exhaust megaphone whose opening I sliced at a 45-degree angle. This exhaust trumpet echoed a four-cylinder fanfare that must have annoyed my brother's neighbors when I rolled into the driveway, but they never complained.

Crossing the High Plains in a low-powered, four-cylinder car with a loud exhaust wasn't exactly pleasant, especially in the heat of the day. Air conditioning didn't exist for my aging Volvo. I don't even remember whether the radio worked. If it did, the exhaust drowned it out.

Because the car was old, I rarely drove it faster than 55 miles per hour, and that was at a time when the speed limit on the Kansas Turnpike was 80 mph. I dropped Susan at MU in Columbia, Mo., for her senior year, and I soon found a job at the *St. Francois County Daily Journal* in Flat River, Mo. Driving from Flat River to Columbia on weekends extracted quite a toll on the Volvo, and in a matter of months it began to give out. One night the lights went out at 50 mph.

It was obvious that my Volvo wasn't going to survive, and it was hard to resist the appeal of a showroom-fresh Volkswagen Beetle. Before the snow fell that year, I limped my cranky Volvo into a VW dealer in St. Louis and drove back to Flat River in a sparkling red VW with a sunroof. My car odyssey was just beginning. Little did I know where it would take me.

— by Tom Strongman

'36 Cord 810

Paul Bryant's convertible coupe is one of three Cords he has restored

P aul Bryant was 7 years old when he saw a newspaper photo of the 1936 Cord. It "jumped off the page," he said. He liked Cords so much that he would ride his bike to Tadlock's Garage near 43rd Street and Mission Road just to glimpse one. The Cord left an image on his soul that has blossomed into a lifelong association with this unusual automobile.

Bryant, of Prairie Village, Kan., is a retired physics professor from the University of Missouri–Kansas City, and his life has become intertwined with Cords in ways he would never have imagined when he saw his first picture.

He bought a supercharged 1936 Cord Model 810 convertible coupe more than 40 years ago. Bryant's smile widens as he describes how he came to own it.

"I spent nine months courting that Cord," Bryant said, but he had difficulty coming to terms with the owner. One day the owner called. "You haven't been over to see the car for a while," he said. "If you don't come, I'm going to run an ad and sell it."

Bryant and his wife, Martha, met with the owner. They discussed various prices but couldn't agree. The owner's wife, however, was intent on getting her husband to sell the car, so she broke the impasse by strongly urging her husband to accept a compromise price.

The Cord's engine didn't run, and the car needed restoration. Bryant repaired the engine and had the body repainted. Rick Hulett silk-screened new faces for the gauges and re-upholstered the interior. In 1965, after three years of work, he and Martha drove the just-finished Cord to the annual Auburn Cord Duesenberg Festival in Auburn, Ind.

Approximately 150 Cord convertible coupes were built, and about 57 of them were supercharged. Bryant lent his car to the National

Paul and Martha Bryant have been involved with their Cord for more than 40 years. They giggle like kids when they take it for a drive.

Automotive and Truck Museum of the United States in Auburn, for six years, but now it's back home.

Sitting in a museum had not been kind to the Cord. Bryant took it to Stan Gilliland's Auburn/Cord Parts restoration shop in Wellington, Kan., and began the automotive equivalent of CPR. The brakes were repaired, the shift linkage was rejuvenated, and the engine was given a once over. Its heart now beats a steady rhythm once again. The 40-year-old restoration has a lovely patina. Bryant's car is not a trailer queen, but rather one that he and Martha can comfortably drive any time.

When Bryant slides behind the wheel of his convertible coupe with Martha at his side, his grin is as wide as the cockpit. His affection for both is obvious. This trio has been together for so long that the car seems like part of the family. It probably is. ■

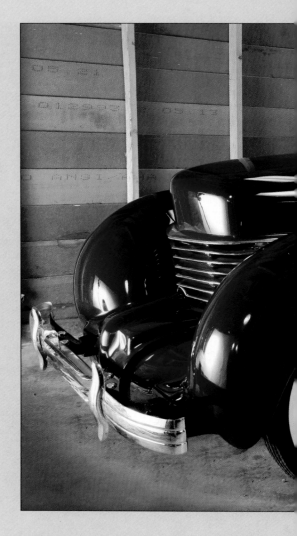

Coppertone Cord

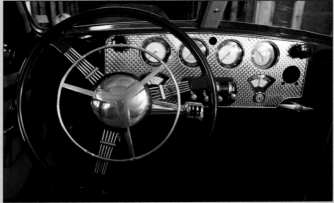

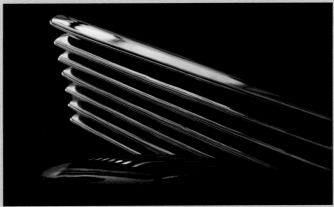

The Coppertone Cord was one of the original prototypes. Bryant has brought it back to like-new condition through hours of patience and hard work.

Paul Bryant has also restored two Cord prototypes: the magnificent E-1 limousine and Gordon Buehrig's Coppertone Cord.

The Coppertone Cord is significant because it was one of the original prototypes of Buehrig's design for a high-performance, front-wheel-drive sedan.

When Bryant found the car in a shed near Minden Mines, Mo., he had no idea it was one of the hand-built prototypes. As the restoration progressed, he realized that many elements of the car were slightly different from a standard 812 Beverly. Puzzled, he called Gordon Buehrig, and Buehrig stopped in Kansas City while driving cross-country. After close examination, he verified that this was, indeed, one of the earliest prototypes. Bryant asked how he should restore the car. "Just as I designed it," Buehrig said.

The restoration has been a long and intermittent undertaking, but Coppertone, as it's known, is almost ready for display. The louvers and wheels are copper-plated like the original show car, and the headlights open from the inside of the fenders rather than the front, as of those of the regular production models. ∎

'64 Corvette

Frank Ellis fell in love with his wife and a car

On Saturday, May 2, 1964, Frank Ellis was competing in the citywide track meet at Noyes Field in St. Joseph, Mo. Ellis was on the track team of Christian Brothers High School, and his steady girlfriend, Carmen Guardado, a student at Bishop LeBlond High School, had been selected as the track queen. He was to be her escort.

After competing in one event earlier in the day, he raced to his school to change clothes and came back to the field. When Guardado rode into the stadium in a Daytona Blue 1964 Corvette con-

vertible, Ellis said he wasn't sure which took his breath away first, the car or the girl, but "when I saw the car, I flipped out."

The image of that dark blue Corvette was irresistible. Many popular songs of that era, such as "Blue on Blue," "Blue Velvet," "Blue Bayou," "Wedding Bell Blues" and "Crystal Blue Persuasion," only reinforced his memory. It was, he said, as if he were haunted by that car.

After dating for six years, Ellis and Guardado married. The bridesmaids' dresses were dark blue. Like the Corvette.

The couple moved to Kansas City, and both went to work for Hallmark. One day in early 1986 Ellis saw a 1964 Corvette while he was sitting at a traffic light. "It was a white convertible with a son and dad in it," Ellis recounts, "and I watched it in my rearview mirror until it went out of sight. I said to myself, 'I'm going to get that car.'"

Ellis studied price guides and talked with friends. The more he talked about the car, the more his "Corvette fever" grew. He found a '64 sitting on a farm in Knob Noster, Mo. It was red, and it needed some restoration, but Ellis figured he could change the color. The owner chuckled and said the original color had been Daytona Blue. Ellis discovered the car was built in the same month and year that he started going steady with Guardado. He bought the car and had it painted Daytona Blue before he took it home.

"That car has not had a drop of rain on it since we bought it," Carmen said. "When we go somewhere, he parks the furthest away."

Ellis, whose great-great-grandfather Joseph Robidoux was the founder of St. Joseph, loves driving his Corvette back to St. Joe to cruise old haunts. When he does, the days of his youth, filled

with so much excitement and possibility, seem close at hand. Every trip in the Corvette also reminds him of that beautiful day in May, more than 40 years ago, when his life took a turn that forever bonded him with his wife and a Corvette.

"Whenever I drive this car," he said, "I think of Carmen, and I think of us." ∎

When Frank Ellis saw Carmen ride into the stadium atop a Daytona Blue 1964 Corvette, he said he wasn't sure which took his breath away first, the car or the girl. When he found this Corvette it was red, but it had originally been Daytona Blue. He had it painted.

'63 Ford F-100

The Miles family loves Old Green

The Miles' family farmland northwest of Mound City, Mo., has a magnetism you can almost feel. The red-and-white barn that great-grandpa Miles built with timber from the land sparkles today just as it did in 1896. The hills look like green waves in an ocean of earth.

It was across these fields that Susan and Lori Miles first learned to drive Old Green, a 1963 Ford F-100. They were so young that they couldn't steer and reach the pedals at the same time. Their dad, Melvin, would put the truck in granny gear, and they would bump across the stubble, while he stood in back and shoveled hay to the cows in winter. At the edge of the field, he would slide back in and drive home.

The Miles family has been here for five generations, and they are as much a part of the landscape as the fertile fields and ever-changing skies. Melvin Miles' dad took his first breath, and his last, in the northwest bedroom of the farmhouse where Melvin's daughter Lori now lives with her husband, Gregg Smith, and children Miles and Leslie. Melvin and Thelma, or TJ as she's known, live around the corner.

Susan and husband Tim Mattson live near Maryville with their sons, Nic and Tate.

The lifelong continuity that is so much a part of the Mileses life is manifest in the pick-up truck that Melvin's dad bought new for $1,944. Like Melvin

Melvin and TJ Miles have kept Old Green on their family farm since his dad bought it new. Daughters Susan and Lori learned to drive in it. Now that the truck has been restored, grandson Miles Smith often takes it to car shows.

and his forefathers, this truck has spent its entire life on the family farm.

Old Green has never let Melvin down. One day, while trying to get out of a muddy field, he worked the truck so hard that his cousin, O'Neil Miles, said he could hear the straight pipes howling at his farm two miles away.

A farm truck is a workhorse, and after decades it deserved some rest. About 10 years ago Melvin took his truck to Pitzenberger's Auto Body in Maryville. What started as a minor repair job evolved into a full-blown restoration that took nearly five years.

Today, Old Green is a family treasure. It looks as if it just rolled off the assembly line. The engine ticks over like a sewing machine. Grandson Miles Smith often takes it to car shows and small-town parades.

But most of all, Old Green is a metaphor for the powerful forces that connect the Miles family to one another and these rolling hills of Missouri. Once there, it's hard to leave. ■

'86 Camelot Model A

Rosalie Burton's Model A replica brightened her last days

It is fitting that Rosalie Burton's Model A replica was made by the Camelot Motor Car Co. "Camelot" is defined as a place or situation that is enlightened, cultured, beautiful and peaceful.

In the last few months of Burton's struggle with cancer, her car brought her a beauty and peace that tasted even sweeter because of the fight against her disease.

Burton and her husband of 35 years, Lance, loved Model A's. They were members of the Heart of America Model A Club, and also have a 1930 Fordor Town Sedan and a 1928 AR Sport Coupe. She enjoyed touring in the Fordor and the Burtons would often drive their 1930 Fordor halfway across the country for a Model A gathering.

Burton couldn't drive her husband's Model A's because they have manual transmissions, so she figured a Model A replica would be ideal because it has a four-cylinder engine and an automatic transmission from a Ford Pinto and a front suspension from a Mustang II.

The Camelot Motor Car Co. came into existence when it bought the assets of the bankrupt Shay Car Co. in the early 1980s. Shay developed a line of Model A replicas that used a custom frame and modern components. Camelot went out of business in 1986.

Burton, of Raymore, located this Camelot Phaeton in Sparta, Mich. Most of the Shay and Camelot cars were roadsters, so her Phaeton is quite rare. She named it Katie after one of her granddaughters.

Burton loved showing her car, and she often used club activities as short-term goals during the waning months of her cancer fight. Many women from the club visited and took her for treatments. Burton felt, Lance said, that long-term goals weren't realistic, but "anybody with their next goal only a week away can make that." Burton lived considerably longer than her doctors predicted, and Lance said he felt that was due in part to her interest in the club activities.

Burton died in February, 2006, and more than 200 friends, many of them from the Model A Club, attended the funeral. ∎

Lance and Rosalie Burton shared a love of Model A Fords that carried over into her fight with cancer. She often used club events as short-term goals.

'65 Corvette

Dana Forrester's hobby blossoms into a business

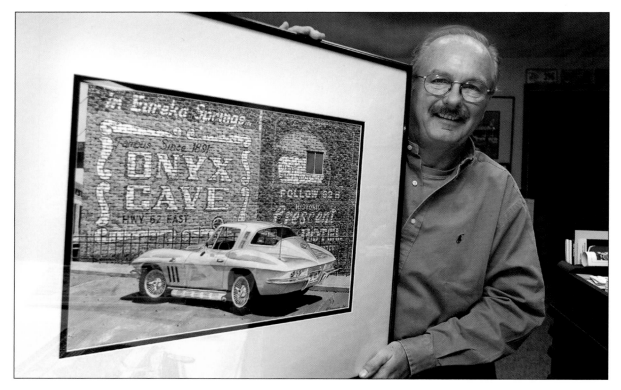

Dana Forrester's painting of his '65 Corvette Sting Ray coupe is called Silver Bullet.

Corvettes are Dana Forrester's hobby, and painting pictures of them is his occupation. If you've ever been to the Plaza Art Fair, you've seen his signature paintings of Corvettes placed in front of brick walls adorned with nostalgic signs.

Forrester, of Independence, started concentrating on automotive artwork in 1990, and today his pieces have made him a well-known part of the national Corvette landscape. He is immersed in Corvettes, and his studio is chock-a-block with enough models, paintings and automobilia to start a small museum. He spends between 75 and 150 hours creating each of his limited edition pieces. When the 700 lithographs are sold there are no more.

"I'm in life to have fun, and I'm so fortunate to be able to paint what I want," he said.

Forrester's love for Chevrolet's fiberglass sports car goes beyond his artwork. He has two Corvettes of his own, including the one he calls Silver Bullet, a rare 1965 Sting Ray coupe with a 425-horse, 396-cubic-inch engine. The Sting Ray has always had a special place in his heart. He saw his first one when he was in junior high school. "I wasn't interested in cars until I saw that," he said.

Forrester said that approximately 2,157 big-block 'Vettes were built at the end of 1965, and his car is a stunning example. Originally sold by Glenn Rapp Chevrolet in Marion, S.D., it is equipped with every option except power windows, including knock-off aluminum wheels and a teak steering wheel.

His Silver Bullet is amazingly like it was when new. One of its previous owners put clear coat over the original paint, and the engine was overhauled in 1994. Forrester says his car is about 94 percent original. In a show, it was just short of scoring a Top Flight award by the National Corvette Restorers Society.

Forrester bought his car in 1997, and it had just over 51,000 miles. He has driven it about 13,000 miles, and the odometer, he says, has just passed his ZIP code.

Sting Rays built between 1963 and 1967 are some of the most sought-after Corvettes. Their futuristic design was a benchmark for 1960s car design, and the chassis was much improved over the earlier models.

Forrester's Sting Ray has been immortalized in one of his paintings, labeled "Silver Bullet." "I've never forgotten the sculptural shape of the back of that car," Forrester said, and that is the angle that is most prominent in his painting. ■

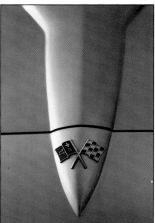

A Sting Ray's tail is among its most recognizable features. The hood bulge is shaped like a rocket.

'52 MG TD

Al Hager bids his MG adieu after nearly 50 years

Al Hager's pale yellow 1952 MG TD is as much a part of his character as the jaunty wool cap and mile-wide grin he wore when he drove it for the last time.

Hager fell in love with MGs while attending the University of Edinburgh in the early 1950s. He became the senior pastor of Asbury United Methodist Church in Prairie Village, Kan., in 1955, and a couple of years later parishioner Bob Grimes found this MG for Hager.

Since 1957, this perky little two-seater has been intertwined with his family's history almost like a person. Hager, his wife, Dot, and sons Jim and Steve came of age with this car. "All of us would pile into the MG: Steve and Dixie the boxer dog behind the front seat, Jim on a pillow atop the emergency brake, while Dot and I occupied the seats," Hager said.

The four Hagers cruising through a budding Prairie Village in their MG typified the innocence and optimism of the late 1950s. The neighborhood around 75th Street and Nall Avenue was bustling with young people, and Hager's church blossomed. He was the pastor there for 26 years.

Dot, Jim, Al and Steve Hager have been MG enthusiasts since 1957. Al's first MG was a pale yellow 1952 MG TD. All four of them used to pile in for drives through suburban Prairie Village.

Hager's sons grew up loving MGs. They helped their dad work on the MG, and the whole family belonged to the MG T-Series Club. When Steve went to Baker University, Hager promised him an MG TD if he kept his grades "top notch." Steve came home in April 1971. Eager to see his car, he looked into the garage and found a frame, an engine, four wheels and more than 40 boxes of parts.

"We went to work," Steve said, and three years later, he had a restored 1953 MG TD. "Steve spent his money on the car instead of pop and girls," Hager said.

Jim Hager bought his 1954 MG TF when he was a student at Baker. He and his grandfather pulled it home from California behind a 1955 Ford Thunderbird.

After all these years, Hager finally sold his beloved MG to a buyer from Vienna, Austria.

Before the car headed overseas, the family gathered to photograph their three cars together for the last time.

For nearly two hours, the Hagers grinned and laughed and nudged one another. Tops were folded, chrome wiped off and hats put on. Cameras snapped constantly as family members recorded the occasion.

As the afternoon shadows lengthened, the stories were told and retold. After the group dispersed, Hager drove his little yellow MG across town and handed the keys to the person who is shipping it overseas. "It came from overseas," he said, "and now it's going back."

For Hager, parting with his car was almost like losing a loved one. The memories it has given will always be larger than life. Its body may be gone, but its spirit lives forever. ∎

Jim, left, Steve, center, and Al gathered their three MGs for one last time before Al sent his car to a buyer in Austria. Steve's car is a 1953 TD, while Jim's is a 1954 TF.

'63 Chevy

Driving down a 40-year-old memory lane

Peggy fed Dave a piece of anniversary cake at the culmination of their 40th anniversary ride in their 1963 Chevrolet.

Dave Wakefield was almost late to his wedding 40 years ago. He is a barber and that September Saturday was especially busy. Many of his customers jokingly tried to make him late by coming in for shaves at the end of the day.

Wakefield flew out of the shop, grabbed a quick bath and burned up the road from Mound City to the church in Mapleton, Kan., in his '63 Chevy Impala Super Sport 409. He arrived with five minutes to spare. Folks said they could hear him coming when he was four miles away. That was, he said, one of the few times he redlined the 409.

On Sept. 3 of 2006, while a handful of friends and family watched, Wakefield and his wife, Peggy, wound the clock back 40 years and cruised down Mound City's main drag in that very same Impala Super Sport. Tied onto the back bumper was the very same string of seven cans that friends put on their car on their wedding night.

Dave has been a barber for 49 years, and he and Peggy have been in the same house for 39 years. Change is not taken lightly.

Wakefield bought his Chevy from the dealer in Mound City. The sticker price was $3,573. He sold the car in 1973 when he and Peggy needed a family-friendly car, and in 1983 it went to a woman in Mulvane, Kan. Last summer, Peggy decided to surprise her husband for his 65th birthday, and she bought the car back over the phone, sight unseen.

Peggy couldn't believe how bad the

car looked when she saw it. The body had no dents and a minimum of rust, but the paint was peeling and the interior was a mess. The car needed a frame-off restoration. The Wakefields took their car to Tim Riegel and Brian Brewer at Fast Eddie's Hot Rod Shop in Lamar, Mo. The body and frame were stripped to bare metal and the engine and transmission were overhauled. The body got new Cordovan Brown paint, and the seats were recovered with Saddle Tan upholstery. The seat-upholstery buttons are original, and the original license plate is back in its rightful place.

When the Wakefields cruised their 409 through Mound City on their anniversary, the clanking of those wedding cans was more like the tinkle of a wedding chime. It has been said that in matters of the heart, the most important things are those that you can't see. Dave and Peggy are proof. ■

The cans dragging behind the Wakefield's Chevy are the very same ones that were tied to their bumper 40 years ago. Few people would retain the cans from their wedding, but the Wakefields are unusually sentimental.

AC Bristol

Steve and Ridge Rees bond by building a sports car together

Every night, it's the same ritual for Steve Rees. "I look in the garage when I get home, and this car is a snapshot of our memories." The car is an AC Bristol that Rees and his 18-year-old son, Ridge, restored during the eight months before Ridge left for his freshman year in college.

"It's almost like a shrine," Rees said. "It's our shrine, and it's great."

Steve Rees and his son Ridge turned a "broken and nasty" hulk into a finished car in eight months. Brian Haupt at Carriage and Motor Works refurbished the body while the guys worked on mechanical pieces.

Rees, of Kansas City, Mo., has been fanatical about cars since he was 15. He has owned and raced cars since 1986, the high point being a drive at the 24 Hours of Daytona in 1996. He hasn't raced in recent years. Ridge, during his senior year at Rockhurst High School, told his mom, Jo Beth, he was unhappy that his dad had not shared his car experience. Hearing that, Rees, with the help of Roger Hurst, located this AC Bristol in a barn. Jo Beth said the hulk they hauled home on a trailer was so "broken and nasty" that she thought they were crazy. But the two could look past the mess and see the car within. It helped that Rees' very first vintage racer had been an AC Bristol.

What seems like a typical car restoration story is more than that for Rees and his son. "It was something we could do together," said Ridge, "something he could pass on to me, something that we would have forever. In the end, we have this great car." And something much more. "It was a way to relate," Rees said.

Restoring a car in eight months is a monumental chore, and it took lots of planning. While the body was being refurbished by Brian Haupt at Carriage and Motor Works Inc., Rees and Ridge worked on the mechanical pieces.

Parts arrived in the mail nearly ever day.

Stripping paint, polishing parts and fabricating pieces for the AC was a way for a father and son to learn about each other and about life, and to share a passion. They forged a new kind of relationship. Driven to complete the car before Ridge left for college, father and son tackled some part of the project every day. Sometimes on weekends, Ridge and his dad would start working on the car after Ridge came home from a date, and they would be in the garage until 4 or 5 a.m. They each said there were times when they fell asleep under the car.

"Almost every morning they had something to show as an accomplishment," Jo Beth said.

Working on the car with his dad came at a "wonderful moment when Ridge was transitioning from a young boy to a man," said Jo Beth. "We saw him grow up," she said. He was more disciplined in school and learned to be patient when working on the car. "He was light-years ahead of where he had been before," she said.

In some ways, the project became a metaphor for how fathers and sons change roles. Rees taught Ridge to fabricate aluminum panels, for example, but once he learned, "a lot of times he was better at it than I was. It was like I was going out to pasture and he was coming in," Rees said.

Rees ordered a 345-horsepower V-8 from Ford and installed it in place of the original engine. The result is nearly identical to the original AC Cobra developed by Carroll Shelby.

Ridge and his dad took the car for a quick spin without a hood or a windshield the night before he left for college. Their dream is now a reality that they will keep forever. What they learned about each other will last a lifetime. ∎

'31 Model A Ford

Leon and Marshall Miller collect vintage cars together

Cars are a special bond between Leon Miller and his son, lawyer Marshall Miller. The multiple-car garage that houses their collection is as cozy as a kid's clubhouse.

Miller and his son began collecting cars about five years ago. "We both decided that while we've always been interested in cars, we've never collected any, and neither of us were getting much younger, so we were going to start doing that," Marshall said.

The first car they bought was a green 1931 Model A with black fenders and green wire wheels.

Leon Miller's first new car was almost identical. He bought it when he was a kid just out of high school. It cost $450, and he paid the dealer with a fistful of bills and change from his savings.

Miller has many fond memories of that car. He played trumpet in a dance orchestra and used his Model A to get to engagements. Fellow musicians would often pile into the rumble seat. "Playing for orchestras was fun, but I didn't make much money," he said. Miller eventually quit the band and went to work for his dad.

"Dad drives the Model A every Sunday," Marshall said.

"Only in nice weather," his dad added.

Miller, of Kansas City, is a very active 93-year-old. He has an office with his son and goes to work every day. His office is decorated with model cars, old photos and his old trumpet. He delivers Meals on Wheels every Thursday, and on Friday afternoons he visits cardiac patients at St. Luke's Hospital. He carries pictures of his cars to use as conversation starters.

Miller's other collector car is a 1969 Fiat 500 Autobianchi Giardiniera. He found it in Canada. It was in good condition and needed only a new paint job. The interior is original.

Miller's everyday car is a new Mini Cooper. Marshall chuckled when he said that he suspected his dad was the oldest person ever to buy a Mini Cooper.

Leon Miller is a very active 93-year-old. His office in his son's firm is decorated with model cars, old photos and his old trumpet. He delivers Meals on Wheels every Thursday, and on Friday afternoons he visits cardiac patients at St. Luke's Hospital. He uses photographs of his cars to get hospital patients engaged in conversation.

'39 Zephyr

Marshall Miller's 1939 Lincoln Zephyr four-door convertible has an elegant simplicity and a fluid shape that rivals some French cars of the same period. Art deco automobiles have a smooth, flowing design that gives movement to the energy within. Miller's Zephyr convertible is both rare and beautiful. Only 302 were made. The Zephyr was unusual in its day because it had unibody construction, a 125-inch wheelbase and a 267-cubic-inch flathead V-12 engine that produced 110 horsepower. It also had hydraulic brakes, a centrally mounted gearshift lever and a dashboard dominated by a large, central speedometer surrounded by smaller gauges.

Dreams of Speed

Chapter Three

Old race cars stir my blood like no other. The only photograph I have of my grandfather, John DeBoor, is a fading, fuzzy image of him sitting behind the wheel of a homemade racer of undetermined origin. He was, with twinkling eyes, bright smile and backward cap, clearly in his element.

My grandfather died when I was not much older than a toddler. My memories of him are dim at best, and this photograph is my only connection.

John DeBoor operated an auto shop in the 1930s and 1940s in north-central Illinois. My mom always said my love of cars came from him, and when I look at his picture, the tingle on the back of my neck makes me suspect she was right. One magical summer afternoon more than a decade ago cemented that notion.

I was covering the Great Race for the first time, and Tom McRae, race founder, paced each day's route with a replica of a 1938 Indy racer. He made a grand entry into every day's finish line with spinning wheels, barking exhaust and his white beard fluttering in the wind. It was hard to tell whether McRae was P.T. Barnum or Barney Oldfield. He was probably a little of each

As competitors left the lunch stop in Moses Lake, Wash., McRae, knowing I was new to the event and keen to embed a lasting impression, summoned me into the driver's seat of his black speedster. Its eight-cylinder Buick belched more than 200 horsepower through an exhaust pipe the size of a downspout. We donned black leather aviator helmets and goggles, zipped monogrammed Great Race jackets up to our necks and tied red bandannas across our faces. We looked like stunt pilots.

After the last competitor left town, we hit the road. We were the "pace car," McRae shouted, and we could drive as fast as we wanted. While the rally racers dutifully executed their afternoon route of precision navigating, we blasted by them, fluttering bandannas hiding smiles as wide as the rolling plains of eastern Washington.

Even modern replicas of 1930s are hardly civilized, and McRae's car was typical. The vague steering made the car skittish, and the brakes were only marginally effective at slowing our pace. The nonsynchronized gearbox was a challenge, particularly on downshifts, but I got the hang of double-clutching pretty quickly. McRae's advice on driving his racer: "Don't try to steer it. Let it go where it wants, and just catch it now and then." As I relaxed, I began to enjoy the power and brutality of his racer.

We bobbed and weaved over the wheat-covered landscape, chased by booming exhaust echoes that I can still hear today. One by one we picked off the competing cars, and we stopped for a quick oil-change in Spokane. McRae's engine was dying slowly, and fresh oil kept most of the metallic crud out of the engine.

As we neared the heart of Coeur d'Alene, Idaho, McRae bailed out and made his way to the finish line so he could announce the entrants' arrival. My job, he said, was to wait a couple of minutes and then make a grand entry.

His racer barely squeezed through the cheering crowds that lined the streets. I blipped the throttle, muscled the wheel and felt like a conquering hero as I drove across the finish line. This long afternoon in a vintage race car was a powerful epiphany. Now I understand the twinkle in my grandpa's eyes.

— by Tom Strongman

'34 Ford Indy car

Gary Kuck preserves Pop Dreyer's unique racer

Gary Kuck, left, and Rex Gardner are two-time Great Race champions. Kuck's crew completely rebuilt the old racer so it would be roadworthy for Great Race competition.

Picture this: It's October of 1946 at the Alabama State Fair, and "Antonio the Great" wheels his Rocket Car down the straightaway of the dirt track, tail ablaze with eight Jet Assisted Take Off rockets belching fire and smoke. Over the dust, noise and commotion the announcer screams, "He must be going 650 miles per hour." More like 85 mph, truth be told, but that's showbiz.

Antonio the Great was Andy Granatelli. Granatelli went on to become famous as the head of STP and the owner of the car that Mario Andretti drove to victory at the Indianapolis 500 in 1969.

The Rocket Car was originally built by Pop Dreyer for the 1934 Indy 500 as the Don Hulbert Special. Hulbert was a Chicago Ford dealer, and he commissioned Dreyer to craft the sensational aluminum body with its laidback grille and large dorsal fin. Power came from a Ford flathead V-8.

The 220-cubic-inch V-8 wasn't competitive at Indy, and the car failed to qualify. Granatelli and his two brothers owned a Chicago speed shop, and they bought the car. In 1946, they added the JATO rockets to the tail and sent 23-year-old Andy to

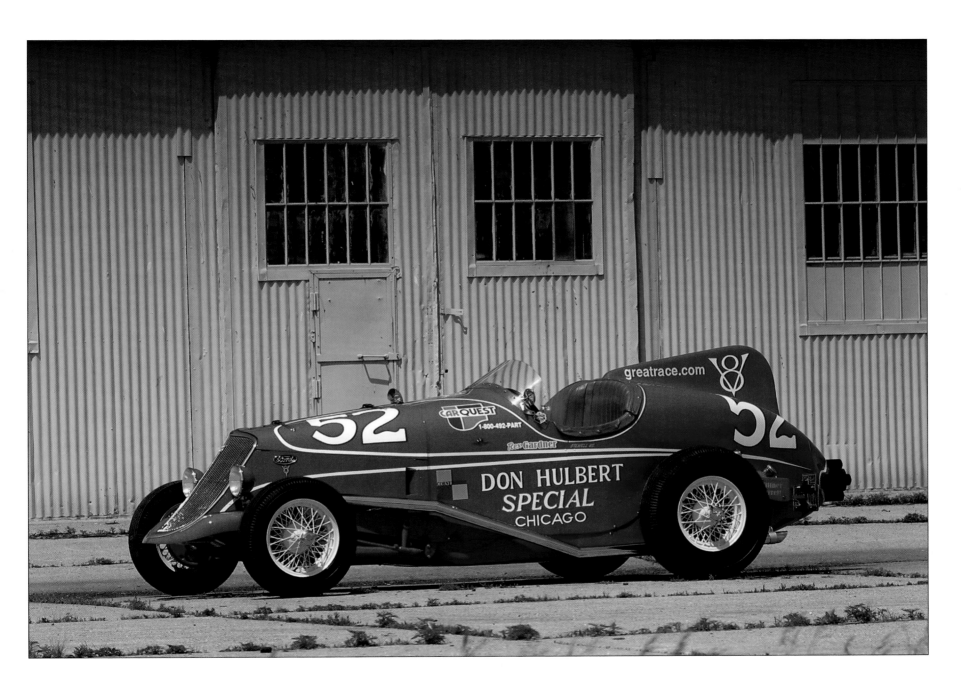

campaign the car at small dirt tracks and county fairs.

In 1983, Stan Betz of Orange, Calif., brought the Rocket Car back to its original condition. Tom McRae of Granbury, Tex., founder of the Great Race, bought it in 1999.

In 2001, Gary Kuck of Lincoln, Neb., purchased the car from McRae to compete in the Great Race. Kuck, and driver Rex Gardner, of Stillwell, Kan., are two-time Great Race champions.

Larry Sittner and Jim Ferrell, friends of Kuck, spent seven months on a complete frame-off restoration, and Gardner built a hot flathead V-8.

After several years of competing in the Great Race, the Rocket Car is now living a life of retirement in Kuck's private collection. ∎

The Great Race is as much a celebration of American values as it is a rally/race for old cars. Because driving out in the open for two weeks requires protection from the sun and wind, Rex Gardner bundled himself in Old Glory. The rocket outlets, above, are fake.

Kuck navigates while Gardner drives. The Great Race is a precision-driving event that rewards consistency and accuracy.

'21 Model T Racer

Phil Tate constructs a copy of his dad's Gallatin Four

In September of 1921, Joe Tate and his Model T speedster were a lap and a half ahead of his competitors at the Hamilton, Mo., track when he crashed.

Tate and his car, the Gallatin Four, were ready to pass fellow racers in front of the grandstand when his racer hit a low spot in the dirt, spun out and plowed through the fence. A two-by-six wooden plank broke his jaw.

Although Joe had been racing for a couple of years, the accident was all it took for his wife to put an end to his escapades. Joe quickly sold his car to someone in Kansas.

Joe Tate owned the Gallatin Motor Co., a Ford dealership. From 1919 to 1921, he had considerable success racing his Gallatin Four on the dirt tracks of northwestern Missouri. His wooden-wheeled two-seater was modified with a shortened frame and lowered suspension. The four-cylinder Model T engine sported a Roof 16-valve cylinder head, lightweight pistons and a counter weighted crankshaft. A two-speed Ruxtel rear end helped Joe outrun his competitors.

Joe Tate's grandson, Phil Tate of Gallatin, Mo., was fascinated with his grandfather's racing and tried to track down the original racer. Tate talked to a mechanic who once worked in his grandfather's shop, and he said the speculation was that when Joe sold his car to a Kansan he reserved the right to drive it one last time. For two days before and two days after the Kansas State Fair, the mechanic said, Joe Tate mysteriously disappeared.

Phil Tate assumes his grandfather had one last race without his wife's knowledge.

Unable to find the original car, Phil Tate decided to build a replica.

Tate began the re-creation of his grandfather's car from "nothing but a torn and incomplete picture and word-of-mouth stories. It stands," he wrote, "as a

This torn photograph was the only thing Phil Tate had to use as a reference to build a copy of his grandfather's racer. The result is as true to the original as he could make it.

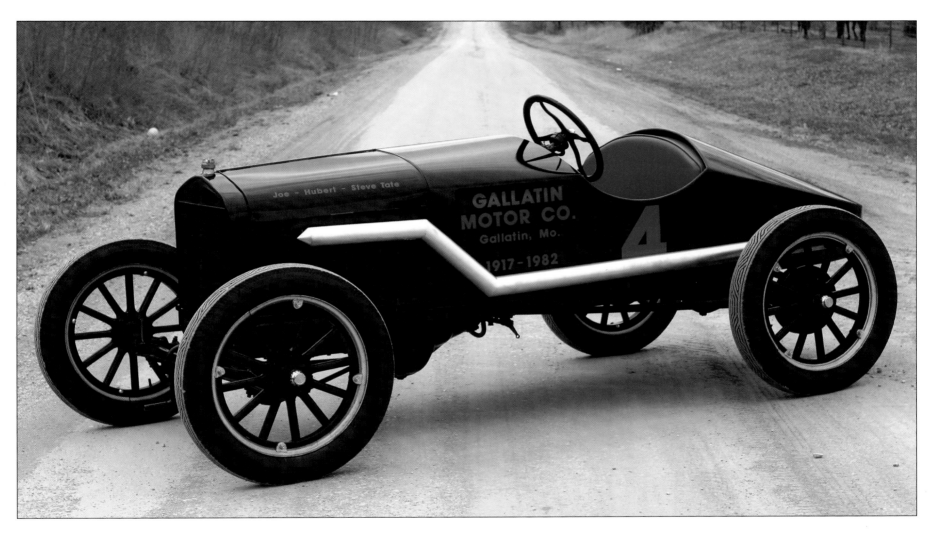

memorial to three really fine men (Joe, Hubert and Steve Tate) and it embodies both the spirit and the contribution that their company, the Gallatin Motor Co., and their family made to this region of the state." Steve Tate died in 2005.

Tate started with a restored chassis and running gear that he bought in the early 1990s. He pored over books to learn how Model T speedsters were constructed and spent nearly 10 years track-ing down parts and designing a body. He constructed a balsa-wood model and formed a body out of stiff paper. Jim Wilson of Wilson Rods in Moberly, Mo., built the body based on Tate's model.

Tate plans to install a Roof 16-valve cylinder head, Winfield carburetor and a re-routed exhaust. Then he will add names and numbers to more closely replicate a fairground racer.

Tate said he may some day donate his car to a museum as an appropriate testament to his brother, father and grandfather and the business they built in Northern Missouri. But for now, he gets a kick out of firing up his Model T speedster and letting its wide-open exhaust echo once again through the town where the original Gallatin Four was born. ■

'65 Porsche Carrera GTS 904

Robert Serra's sleek racer was a watershed car

Robert Serra of Kansas City, Kan., relishes his Porsche 904 like an art connoisseur cherishes great artwork, partly because it is one of the last ones built, and partly because it is such a historically significant car. The fact that it's fast, sleek and viscerally exciting is an added bonus.

Serra, a Kansas district judge in Wyandotte County and an honorary vice consul of Italy, is a longtime Porsche enthusiast.

The Carrera GTS Type 904 was the first Porsche to have a separate chassis, a glass-rein- forced plastic body and a midship-mounted engine. The four-cam, four-cylinder engine pro- duced about 180 horsepower in racing trim.

The 904 prototype was introduced in 1963. It was designed by Ferdinand Alexander "Butzi" Porsche, the grandson of company founder, Ferdinand Porsche. One hundred had to be built in order for it to meet International Automobile Federation regulations for racing. The sleek and aerodynamic body is roughly 42 inches tall and looks as gorgeous today as it did more than 40 years ago. Serra surmises that about 60 904s still exist.

Serra's 904 is a 1965 with serial number 904099. It was delivered on Oct. 15, 1965. Its first owner was Clyde McNeill of Thomas, Okla. Serra bought the car in 1975 from Milton McWilliams of Rockaway, N.J.

Serra has restored the car to its original condi- tion. When he got it, it had the wrong wheels, no

The 904 was the first Porsche to have a separate chassis and a fiberglass body. The engine is mounted in the middle of the car, which was also a first for Porsche. Robert Serra has owned his car for more than 30 years.

headlight covers, no underbody pans and a missing muffler shield, but all of those items are intact once again. With its dark blue upholstery and silver paint, it looks just as it did back in 1965.

Since the 904 weighs about 1,350 pounds, the small engine propelled it to 60 miles per hour in roughly five seconds, and to a top speed of 164 mph. Its first victory was the 12 Hours of Sebring in 1964. A long streak of race wins followed.

Has Serra ever driven it on a track? No. He said he doesn't want to risk it, because it is so rare and valuable. He shows it at Porsche meets and occasionally drives it on the street. Even that is a challenge, he said, because it sits so low that "beer cans and turtles" are road hazards. ■

'52 Kurtis sprint car

Mark Randol created a replica of his dad's famous racer

The symbol of the spirit of Tom Randol sits under a blanket in his son Mark's garage. It has four wheels, has a blue and yellow paint job and is powered by the exact Offenhauser engine from Tom's original 1952 Kurtis sprint car.

Mark Randol of Greenwood, Mo., commissioned a replica of his dad's car.

Tom Randol's involvement in dirt track racing dates to the late 1930s when he used his excavating company's heavy equipment to bank the track at Olympic Stadium, a small oval located near today's intersection of Truman Road and Interstate 435. After the war, Tom Randol bought a midget racer, and, with Bob Slater of Kansas City driving, it won the track championship in 1951. Slater talked Randol into ordering a new Kurtis sprint car and an Offenhauser engine for the 1952 season. The car and the engine each cost $6,000.

Tom Randol's sprint car won its first race in July of 1952. Slater drove it to victory in its first International Motor Contest Association race in

Mark Randol remembered his dad's famous racer, far right page, and commissioned a replica. Don Brown built the car and A.J. Watson helped with the engine, which is the exact same one used in the original car. The Kurtis sprint car is a picture of raw power even when sitting quietly.

Lincoln, Neb. Mark Randol still has the trophy. Randol and Slater won 11 of 21 IMCA races that year and finished fourth in the points standing. Slater campaigned his own car the next year, winning the championship in 1953 and 1954. Slater died in a crash in 1955. His wife, now Mary Lou McClure, remarried and lives today in Raytown.

Mark Randol had trophies, clippings, photos and other memorabilia from his dad's days as a race car owner. The only thing missing was the car. He traced his dad's original car through numerous owners until it seemed to drop from sight. "It probably ended up in a boneyard," he said. He did secure some of the original parts, such as the steering wheel, the rear axle, a couple of side panels and the front spindles. With that, he commissioned Don Brown of Indianapolis to build a replica. The legendary A.J. Watson helped with the engine.

The Kurtis sprint car had an 86-inch wheelbase and weighed from 1,300 to 1,400 pounds. Only five or six were ever made. The four-cylinder, 270 Offenhauser engine produced about 350-400 horsepower. Sprint cars were fast, and dangerous. Many drivers died in crashes.

Don Brown re-created the Kurtis from a photograph that Mark Randol had enlarged so that it could be used to make 1/4-scale drawings. Brown created the body completely by hand out of aluminum, and the grille alone is a work of art. Once the car was back in Kansas City, Cunningham Auto Body did the paint and Bob Bond the lettering.

In a twist of good fortune, Mark Randol located the original engine from his dad's car, serial number 160, in Kentucky. It was little more than a box of parts. Randol patiently rebuilt the engine in his basement. On the day after Christmas 2002, he loaded the engine into his truck and drove it to Watson's garage in Indianapolis. Watson put it on the dyno and began coaxing Offy No. 160 to run.

Mark Randol said that watching his engine belch to life after being silent for nearly 40 years was an "unbelievable feeling." It was, he said, a fantastic Christmas present.

For now, Tom Randol's Offy is mute, but when Mark Randol runs his hand across the same steering wheel that Bob Slater grabbed back in 1952, the sounds of yesterday are deafening. ■

Pupulidy Special

John Muller preserves an unusual racer

Brian Haupt, left, of Carriage and Motor Works was instrumental in putting John Muller's Pupulidy Special back together in excellent condition.

The Pupulidy Special has only one seat, but when John Muller drives it in a vintage sports car race, he knows the spirit of Emil Pupulidy is riding with him.

Pupulidy grew up on Long Island and built P-47 fighter planes for Republic Aviation in the 1950s. He raced motorcycles and loved fast cars. While traveling in Europe in 1952, he visited the Porsche factory and bought a brand-new Porsche coupe. He shipped it home and raced it in local events.

In 1953, Pupulidy decided to build a sports car of his own, and he fashioned it after the stream-lined Mercedes-Benz racers he had watched in Europe. He designed a shapely fiberglass body and mounted it on a modified Volkswagen chassis. He called it the "Beast," and it won its first race in 1954 at the Nassau Speed Weeks in the Bahamas. The curvaceous body was quite heavy, so Pupulidy took it off and made a lighter one.

In late 1955, Pupulidy turned his attention to another streamlined body. He created a tube-framed chassis, stamped it PUP 1, and installed a Porsche engine. He sold the car without racing it. PUP 1 had several owners and even sat abandoned behind a New Jersey gas station for a while.

Muller, of Kansas City, saw the unusual little car while browsing through the race car section

of *Hemmings Motor News* in 2003. Even though he didn't know exactly what it was, he knew instinctively that it was worth preserving. He bought it from Matt Willoman in Croton-on-Hudson, New York.

The car was in pretty dismal shape, and Muller turned to a friend, Brian Haupt of Carriage and Motor Works in Kansas City, for a complete restoration. Haupt replaced many of the rusted frame tubes and fabricated a lighter weight fiberglass body after creating a mold from the original. Muller then had Cox Motorsports of Kansas City install a 1600cc Porsche engine. He calls the car "the Pupper."

Muller, who started racing vintage sports cars

in 1988, has a special affinity for unique sports racers. He had Haupt restore a one-off 1957 Tojeiro and a Cooper-Porsche nicknamed "the Pooper."

In 1999, Muller was injured while racing the Pooper. At the urging of his wife, Kathy, he hung up his helmet for a while and sold the Pooper. Now he races the Pupper three or four times a year. Muller and his wife are founders of the Muller + Company ad agency.

Old race cars are pure art to Muller, and he loves bringing them back to life. In 2006 he won first overall in a vintage race at Laguna Seca, Calif. Emil Pupulidy's dream continues to be successful on the track. ∎

When John Muller slides into the Pupper's narrow seat, the spirit of Emil Pupulidy rides along.

Emil Pupulidy's design was inspired by Mercedes-Benz racers of the 1950s, and the body he created for his racer reflects their streamlining.

'37 Delahaye

Cars were a connection between Dr. John L. Baeke and his dad

John L. Baeke drove while his dad, John O. Baeke, navigated during the 1995 Great American Race. The pair spent many hours in preparation for the cross-country rally for vintage cars.

Cars have connected Dr. John L. Baeke and his dad, Dr. John O. Baeke, like an umbilical cord. Their shared passion began with Pinewood Derby cars and led to the restoration of a 1937 Delahaye nearly 30 years later.

They called themselves the Baeke Boys when they competed in the Great American Race in 1995. Leather aviator caps snugged over their ears, the Baekes looked like barnstorming racers from the 1930s as they scrunched into the tiny open cockpit of their racer.

When the Baekes decided to enter the race, they needed a suitable car. They found a Delahaye at an auction in 1994. The spidery Delahaye was, the younger Baeke said with a laugh, "in museum condition." That means it looked great but didn't run well. This stunning racer needed a top-to-bottom mechanical restoration for the Great American Race.

Stan Gilliland of Wellington, Kan., well-known Cord restorer and family friend, brought the Delahaye back to health.

For months, the Baekes prepared for the race. They made lists, gathered parts and drove repeated trips up and down a deserted Kansas highway to perfect their timekeeping. The young Baeke said preparing for the race was almost more fun than the event itself. During the two-week-long time-distance rally for old cars, the

doctors manhandled the Delahaye from Canada to Mexico City through rain and heat. They finished in sixth place.

In 1999, the elder Baeke had a subdural hematoma that left him partly paralyzed after being in a coma for four months. John L. Baeke and his wife, Suzanne, brought his dad into their house for 24-hour care.

"My dad is my best friend," Baeke said. "We're both doctors, and I still go to him for advice."

The elder Baeke's room was on the lower level of his son's home, next to a walk-out family room that was decorated with auto posters and bits of memorabilia from the Great American Race. The most impressive decoration was the Delahaye itself. It sat in the family room so the elder Baeke could see it every time he was wheeled out of his room.

The Delahaye was like a pet that slept outside its master's room, and it kept watch over the memories of the Baeke Boys until the elder Baeke died in 2005. ∎

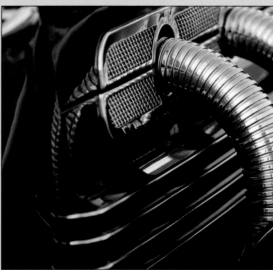

The Delahaye's sleek body gives it a feeling of speed even when it is sitting still. When his father became ill, John L. Baeke parked the Delahaye in the basement family room so his dad could see it every day.

'37 Cord

Dr. John O. Baeke's fascination with Cords began when one nearly ran him down as a young man.

"He was a Depression-era baby. His folks were so poor that his graduation present in 1937 was permission to hitchhike from Clay Center, Kan., to Lincoln, Neb., to visit his uncle," said his son, Dr. John L. Baeke.

While Baeke was in Lincoln, a Cord charged out of a garage and crossed the sidewalk right in front of him. Baeke dived to keep from getting hit, and as he was lying on the ground, he looked back to see a big car with chrome pipes.

The image of those chrome pipes surfaced again in the late 1950s. Dr. John O. Baeke saw a story about Cords, and he immediately focused on the chrome pipes. The flood of memories triggered a search for the Cord he found in California. He flew to Santa Ana to check it out. That's where he saw the car was being used to house chickens. He bought it on the spot. To be sure no one swiped the supercharger, he removed it and carried it home in his lap on the plane.

The car came to Kansas City by truck. John L. Baeke remembers going to the freight terminal to pick up the car with his dad when he was about 8 years old. "That was better than Christmas," he said.

Young Baeke didn't know anything about a Cord, but, "it was a car, it had four wheels, and I was going to get to work on it with my dad." ∎

John O. Baeke discovered this Cord in a field in Santa Ana, Calif., where it was being used to house chickens. He brought the car back to Kansas City for restoration. The car still looks good more than 30 years after its restoration.

'39 Lagonda

A road-going replica of a famous Le Mans racer

Rich Morrison's 1939 Lagonda Le Mans replica looks as if it should be blazing down the Mulsanne straight at the 24 Hours of Le Mans, France, instead of meandering the streets of Salina, Kansas.

Morrison's car is one of fewer than 20 reproductions of the two cars that finished third and fourth in the 1939 Le Mans race. It looks and sounds fierce, but it is surprisingly docile when driven on the street.

Morrison, whose older brother Roger also col-

lects cars, has been hooked on cars for as long as he can remember. He got a go-kart when he was in junior high. His first foray into vintage racing was in 1983 when he drove his 1964 Ferrari 250 GT Lusso in Kansas City's Folly Classic Vintage Grand Prix. Today he races both a vintage Bentley and the Lagonda.

In 1939, the two Lagonda Le Mans racers finished third and fourth in the 24-hour race. These V-12 beauties sprang from W.O. Bentley, the engineer who left Bentley and Rolls-Royce to work for Lagonda in 1935.

Morrison's admiration for Bentley led him to purchase the Lagonda while on a trip to England more than 20 years ago. Morrison said he had just finished reading Bentley's autobiography about his Le Mans exploits when he saw this car for sale in England, and he bought it on the spot. Morrison's replica was built by Joe Harding, formerly of

England and now of San Diego.

Because the actual Le Mans-winning Lagondas were damaged in World War II, replicas such as this one are the only way to get a taste of what the 1939 cars were like. The engine is a 4.5-liter V-12, and Morrison said his car develops 165 horsepower at the rear wheels. Morrison added an overdrive to the four-speed transmission and he said he can comfortably cruise at 70 miles per hour.

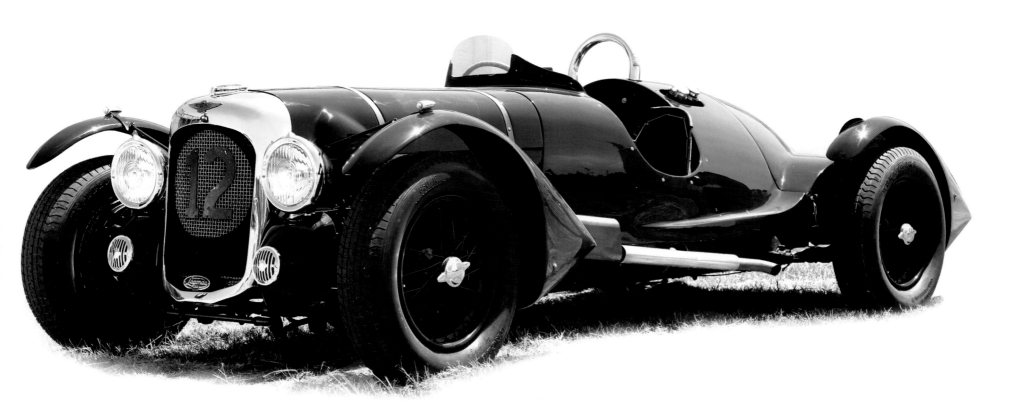

And cruise it he does. Morrison has driven his Lagonda in the Colorado Grand vintage tour twice, and earlier in 2006 he and his wife, Sallie, took it on a 500-mile, three-day tour in West Virginia. He has also raced it up Pikes Peak and twice was given the performance and presentation award at the Monterey Historics race in Laguna Seca, Calif. ∎

Morrison's replica of the Le Mans Lagonda looks like speed personified. The body is wrapped tightly around the mechanical components for streamlining. The large steering wheel is wrapped with twine for a secure grip.

Dreams of Fun

Chapter Four

First cars are like first kisses. They make your head spin, leave you slightly breathless and won't ever be forgotten. My daughter Kristen's first car, a 1976 Volkswagen Scirocco, was all that, and more.

I often noticed a clean VW parked around the corner, but one day it seemed to have a slightly forlorn tilt. That's when I noticed a For Sale sign in the front window. I drove by without giving it much thought, but then it hit me: Kristen was 16 and ready for a car. The VW was cute, green and available, and I suspected the price would be right.

I rounded up my daughter later that day, and we paid the neighbor a visit. Kristen was not especially car-savvy, but in her mind, the Scirocco had three things going for it: Dark green was one of her favorite colors, the little two-door was cute, and her mom and I seemed willing to buy it.

The Scirocco was the sportier, two-door cousin to the Rabbit, and this one was in better-than-average shape. The owner was reasonably careful with its care, but it was 11 years old and had been driven by a teenager. It needed a new clutch. We agreed on a price that accounted for the clutch repair, and took it home. Shortly thereafter, Kristen left to spend the summer in Germany as a foreign exchange student.

While my daughter was overseas, the Scirocco got a new clutch and I gave the paint a good coat of polish. It shone like a bright, but slightly worn, jewel. When she came home at the end of the summer, she brought her VW a German, black rubber Golf shift knob.

Within a few months, her VW began to acquire the kinds of bumps and scrapes common to new drivers. First came a few scratches down one side, and then a ding on the bumper from sliding on sand and bumping someone in the school parking lot. We did our best to polish out the scratches, but some were pretty deep gouges.

The saddest incident of all came about in the most innocent way. Because the engine used a little oil, I told Kristen to check the oil with each tank of gas. She dutifully performed this task one night, but didn't latch the hood. Predictably, it blew open after driving a few blocks. It was bent grotesquely in front of the windshield. She limped home, and we managed to wrench it more or less back into place. A couple of bungee cords held it down. Not pretty, but effective.

Now that the Scirocco had been christened more than once, the rest of its year was notably unremarkable, until I broke the hatchback window. My son and I were playing catch in the driveway. Poor glove work on my part resulted in a baseball smashing right through the glass. The next day I paid a visit to the local junkyard for new glass.

By the time Kristen was ready for her first year of college, the Scirocco went on the block. It was pretty banged up, but a dad and his son were one of the first to answer my ad.

It was perfect, the dad said, because it needed a lot of work. He told me about the deal he had made with his boy, the same deal his dad had made with him. Dad would buy the car, but the son had to fix it up. Fixing the car created ownership, taught basic mechanical skills and gave the dad and the son a reason to bond. It worked for the dad, and he hoped it would work with his son.

I wished them luck as they drove down the drive. I never did see the car after it was repaired, but I hope it was as memorable to the young man as his first kiss.

-- by Tom Strongman

Amphicars

Amphicar owners take a drive on Water Street

Amphicar drivers are a fun bunch.

At last year's gathering of the International Amphicar Owners Club at Lake Ozark, Mo., they plunged their amphibious little cars down boat ramps and into the water like kids doing cannonballs into a pool. The bigger the splash, the wider their smiles.

It's pretty rare to see one Amphicar, much less a dozen of 'em, but that many gathered at Lake of the Ozarks, hosted by Roger Sallee. Sallee grew up in Chanute, Kan., lived in Lee's Summit and now resides at Lake Ozark. He restores Amphicars as a hobby.

An Amphicar is about the size of an old Volkswagen Beetle, and it was built in Germany from 1961 to 1968. The body is watertight, so long as you remember to lock the doors. The bottom of the car is roughly shaped like a

When a group of Amphicar owners take their cars for a "swim," fun takes top billing. A national meet at Lake of the Ozarks brought more than a dozen of these unusual vehicles together.

boat, and it has two propellers in back.

A special transmission allows the wheels and propellers to be operated either independently or simultaneously. Top speed is about 7 miles per hour on water and 70 mph on land. The front wheels are the rudders when they're in water. Power comes from a 43-horsepower British Herald engine mounted behind the back seat.

About 3,878 Amphicars were built, and 90 percent of them came to the U.S. market. They were more novelty than anything, and many ended up as promotional tools for radio stations and companies. Today, collectors are snapping them up.

If a group of ducks is called a flock and a bunch of geese is called a gaggle, what do you call a flotilla of Amphicars? A party.

Just ask the folks at Bayou Bill's, a Lake Ozark restaurant that was convention central. On a Friday night, as the sun slipped behind the horizon, Ken Richter from Louisiana whipped up a batch of crawfish etouffee on the restaurant's deck while a couple of die-hard Amphicar owners took their cars for one last "swim" around the dock. Amphicar owners don't go boating, they "swim.

"Dave the Wave" Derer from Mendota, Ill., saw his first Amphicar at Santa's Village in Dundee, Ill., when he was just a kid. His fascination with this little car grew and grew until now he has an Amphicar restoration business. So why is the Amphicar so special to him? He chuckled and said, "It floats."

Looking at his website, however, reveals a deeper appreciation. He wrote:

"Years ago when I prayed to God for direction, I would never have guessed the answer would be in

Roger Sallee of Lake Ozark, Mo., dives into the water like a little kid doing a cannonball. Amphicars aren't fast, but they are very seaworthy as long as the doors are kept tightly shut.

the form of an Amphicar.

"The days move by us. Our youth somehow vanishes without saying good-bye. The great thing about being young is the newness of all that comes your way. Then something happens, and you realize it's gone. The Amphicar fills that void. When I drive up to a boat ramp, watching the water spin and move, my heart beats faster, in nervous anticipation. It is a new experience every time. I get younger when I drive in. I get younger when I smile. I get younger when I share the Amphicar."

■

Dust Bowl Replica

Don Cochrane loves to create vehicles that are the product of his imagination

Don Cochrane loves cars and trucks, but he isn't content with just any old vehicle. He likes to create his own, and lately his creativity has been moving him in a new direction. He's fascinated by rust.

"I'm retired," Cochrane said, "and my interest in cars won't go away. I'm up by 6 a.m. and bored by 7:30 unless I have a project to work on. I need to challenge the mind, and I need to challenge the hands. When you're done, it either turns out well or it's a big mistake."

Cochrane, of Independence, is an automotive magician. He stirs together unlikely parts and

Don Cochrane's vehicles spring from his imagination. He often mixes parts and pieces from various cars and trucks to create a specific look. Even though his Dust Bowl Replica looks as if it were built in the 1930s, it has a modern chassis and powertrain for reliability.

pieces of various vehicles to create something only he can imagine. He created a vehicle that looks as if it existed during the Dust Bowl, but it has the frame and mechanical heart of a Ford Courier pickup. "If I use a bolt or part that is new, I put a little muriatic acid on it, and I have a nice coat of brown the next morning," Cochrane said.

Cochrane lined the inside of the roof with street signs, covered the seat with a serape and installed a small wooden house where a truck bed would be. He even built a tiny teardrop trailer for trips.

"I had a wreck in it a few months ago. The guy behind hit me hard. The policeman came out, took one look and said, 'Whoa! Did you suffer any damage?'"

"Yeah, he broke the board on the back of the doghouse," Cochrane said with a laugh. ■

Fascination

Unique auto is the culmination of one man's vision

Dream cars have long held us in their grip. Designers with a vision for the future often seek unusual solutions to building a car.

In 1937, Paul M. Lewis had a peculiar vision for the car of the future. He designed and built a front-wheel-drive, three-wheeled Airomobile. The teardrop body was streamlined and aerodynamic. Despite some interest in the vehicle, the Airomobile never went into production.

Lewis kept dreaming about unusual cars with airplane shapes, and in the late 1960s he designed another radical vehicle called Fascination. A propeller drove the three-wheeled prototype, but the propeller failed during a demonstration run and a Volkswagen engine driving the rear wheels became the source of motivation. A second front wheel was added.

Hoping to produce Fascinations in quantity, Lewis created the Highway Aircraft Corp. Lewis acquired a build-ing in Sidney, Neb., and built three vehicles. Fiberglass bodies were fabricated in Lincoln and shipped to Sidney.

Five Fascinations were built in all, and Keith and Eileen Carpenter of Parker, Colo., own three of them.

So how did the Carpenters discover their first Fascination? On a Sunday morning about 30 years ago, Keith and Eileen spotted a black-and gold, airplane-shaped car at Vern Hagestad's Volkswagen dealership in suburban Denver. The Carpenters whipped a U-turn and went back to check out the weird "car" called the Fascination.

"Boy, I'd like to own that someday," Keith said to Eileen.

About 10 years later, the Carpenters were shar-ing their weekly Sunday breakfast with a friend who told them he bought a very unusual car at a storage auction. He took them to see it, and there, on a trailer, was the same black-and-gold car they had seen 10 years earlier. It was basically intact, but the long tails, although still with the car, had been sawed off because they were too long for the storage facility. The windshield was also cracked.

Their friend put the car back into storage, and the Carpenters bought it when he died of cancer

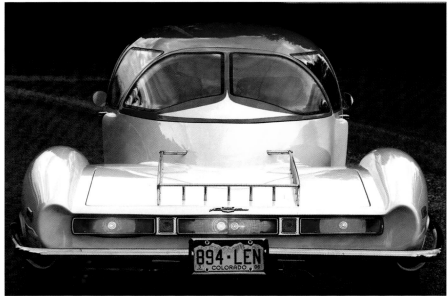

Fascination looks like an airplane without wings. Only five of these unique vehicles were built, and the Carpenters own three of them. They enjoy taking it to car shows all over the country. It runs, but driving it creates a traffic hazard.

20 years ago.

The Carpenters' black-and-gold Fascination is car No. 1, the original prototype that was built in Denver. It is undergoing restoration. The Carpenters have been able to acquire car No. 2 and car No. 3. The red-and-white car that you see here is No. 2, and it is powered by a four-cylinder Renault engine. Cars No. 3 and 4 also had Renault engines. Car No. 5, which the Carpenters also own, has never been fully finished. It has a V-6 engine and the transaxle from an Oldsmobile Toronado.

Car No. 2 spent most of 2005 touring the auto shows such as the Amelia Island Concours d'Elegance in Jacksonville, Fla., Keels and Wheels in Houston, and the Meadowbrook Concours in suburban Detroit.

Do they drive it? "No," Eileen Carpenter said, "it's a trailer queen. We don't drive it because it simply creates too much havoc the way people gawk and pay attention to it." ∎

Fascination's dashboard and curved windshield are more like a light aircraft.

'30 Studebaker

Dean Weller discovers vitality in restoring cars

Dean Weller usually tackles one restoration each year. His garage is overflowing with examples of his handiwork, such as the Buick at right and a 1930 Studebaker, opposite page.

D ean Weller has found the fountain of youth in old cars.

Weller, of De Soto, Kan., is 80 but looks and acts at least 10 years younger. He retired from building homes 27 years ago to concentrate on his car hobby. "Cars were always my thrill, but naturally my family came first, and my wife, Delores, and I had to raise our three daughters before I could ever really get involved."

Since he retired, Weller has restored 23 automobiles, mostly Model A's, in his shop, an old Ford garage in downtown De Soto that was built in 1918. Weller's work routine would wear out a man half his age. During the winter, he spends six days a week in his shop. "Summers are for having

fun with my cars, going on tours, attending swap meets, that sort of thing."

"I'm having fun doing what I want to do. It's 1930 in here. There are no headaches like there are on the street. And working on cars gives me a lot of exercise, which is important. I didn't smoke or drink, and I believe that a little hard work never hurt anyone."

Weller bought the old Ford garage for the showroom and sizable basement storage. He added a two-story addition in back to expand the lower-level storage area and create a south-facing, glass-walled workshop on the upper level. Sun pours into his workspace, providing both light and heat.

Weller is a perfectionist who does all his own

work, with the exception of chrome plating, some machine work and sewing of upholstery. He begins each restoration by painstakingly making three-dimensional drawings of each part as he disassembles the vehicle. The result is a wonderful sketchbook of each restoration, something that is

an invaluable resource.

How did Weller acquire his skills? "They say the way to learn is by trial and error, but I've been very fortunate, " he said, "I've had hardly any errors." His background in building was helpful because he was skilled with his hands and always drew his own blueprints. "If you think things out before you jump into it, you don't usually have to back up too much."

Aside from normal restorations, Weller has created a few cars almost from scratch. He spent 1,000 hours hand-forming a Model A roadster body out of wrought iron so that it looks like metallic lace designed around a theme of "America's sweetheart." He designed and built a woodie body for a Chevrolet, and he also made a Ford panel truck. He designed and built three Model A speedsters.

His shop in De Soto has become a Model A Mecca. He hosts about three seminars each winter. Every Tuesday, from 20 to 30 members of local Model A clubs show up to visit and go to lunch. Weller's basement is cram-packed with hundreds of auto parts, and while they're not for sale, his friends enjoy pawing over them.

Weller said: "I've been very fortunate in my life. I would recommend my footsteps to anybody." ∎

'10 Maytag-Mason

This Iowa car was designed by the legendary Fred Duesenberg

George Hess looked for a Maytag-Mason for 10 years before locating this car in Idaho. Hess admires the Duesenberg's engineering. Fred Duesenberg flipped a racer in Kansas City in 1907.

George Hess gets a wave from almost every car he passes when he's driving his 1910 Maytag-Mason. People can't help responding because it is so unusual to see a car of this vintage, much less see one rolling down the road under its own power.

The Maytag-Mason is a fairly obscure car. The first Mason was designed and built in Des Moines in 1905 by Fred and August Duesenberg. Their car had a two-cylinder, 200-cubic-inch engine mounted under the seat. It produces

between 24 and 28 horsepower. Fred L. Maytag invested in the company in 1909 and moved the factory to Waterloo, Iowa, in 1910. Maytag soon sold his interest in the company and by 1912 the name reverted back to Mason Motor Co. The company went bankrupt in 1915 and was totally out of business by 1917. Approximately 1,500 cars were built, but only about 20 of them exist today. The Everest Kansas Historical Society also has one.

Fred Duesenberg raced a Mason in the 1907 Kansas City hillclimb and nearly ended his career when he flipped it. A Maytag-Mason finished the Glidden Tour in Kansas City in 1909.

Hess, of Lenexa, Kan., has long admired the Mason brand. After 10 years of searching, he found this car. The first buyer was J.D. Hasik of Abie, Neb. Leo Bongers, a collector from David City, Neb., owned it for

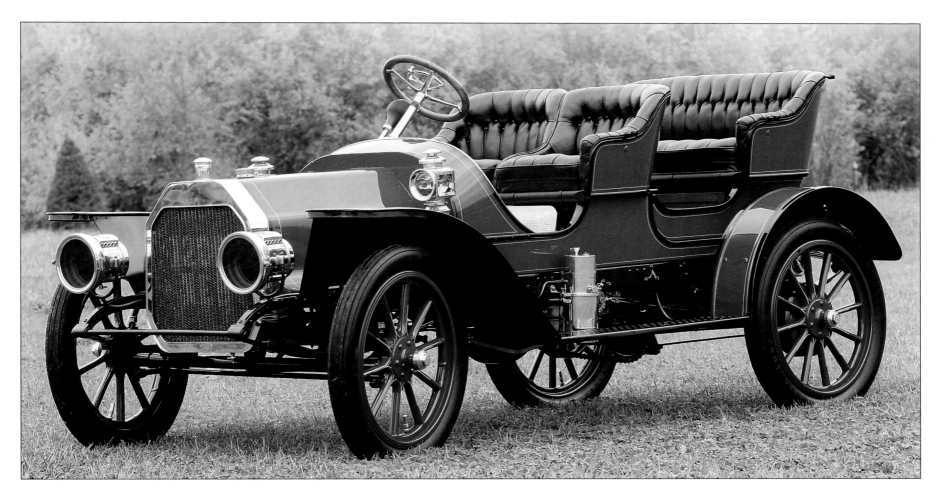

a while. Temple Baldwin of Kimberly, Idaho, got the car from Bongers in 1993 and began a three-year restoration. Hess bought it in August 2003.

The Maytag-Mason is an imposing vehicle. Baldwin's restoration is flawless. The paint looks as if it could have come from the assembly line yesterday. Every detail, from the tiny brass primer cups on each cylinder to the cast aluminum bulkheads, is period perfect. The polished brass lights glisten.

On the day I visited, Hess started his car with two cranks. It idled with the same putt-putt exhaust sound as a two-cylinder tractor or motorcycle. The two-speed transmission gives the car a top speed of more than 40 miles per hour. There is no windshield, and the driver and passengers sit bolt upright in the breeze.

George Hess doesn't mind, however, because he admires Duesenberg's engineering, and nothing pleases him more than taking his Maytag-Mason for a drive.   ∎

'49 Cadillac

Russ Creason enjoys his 'Big Blue' convertible

Russ Creason has long fancied classic convertibles, and this Cadillac is his current fascination. He loves it for the pontoon fenders and the aircraft-inspired styling.

R uss Creason loves classic cars, especially convertibles. He has owned many, including a very rare 1939 Buick Redfern Saloon Tourer, but his current fascination is a 1949 Cadillac Series 62 convertible, which he has nicknamed "Big Blue."

Creason's French Gray convertible is the picture of elegance. It has about 90,000 miles, and much of the car is still original.

Creason, of Kansas City, Mo., worked for General Motors for 31 years. He retired as director of human resources for the international division. Although he is no longer in the car business, he thoroughly enjoys sliding behind the

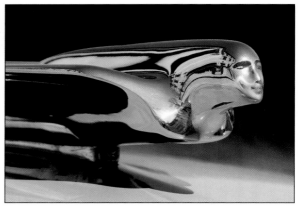

wheel of his ragtop classic for a leisurely drive with his wife, Marge.

Creason is a longtime member of the Classic Car Club of America. He said his friends tease him about owning a 1949 because technically, the "classic" era ends in 1948. Creason bought his car in 1987 at the Kruse Auction in Auburn, Ind., because "1949 was a great year for almost every manufacturer," he said. He loves the Cadillac's design, which was the work of Harley Earl. The pontoon rear fenders and tailfins were inspired by the Lockheed Lightning P-38 fighter plane.

The '49 Cadillac was mechanically revolutionary because its lightweight, 331-cubic-inch V-8 had 160 horsepower. It could push the Caddy to 60 miles per hour in 12.1 seconds and had a top speed of 105 mph.

On the road, Creason's car simply glides along, almost as if the wheels weren't touching the pavement. Creason thinks of his Cadillac as a "man's car," because it is fast, powerful and was inspired by a fighter plane.

"Women all love this car, too," he said, "even if they don't want to drive it." ∎

'51 Mercury

Jack Walker creates a copy of the famous Hirohata custom

Twenty years ago, Jack Walker was driving down Interstate 435 when he passed a 1951 Mercury. He knew immediately that he had to have one. A short time later he found one near Kirksville, Mo. When Walker told the owner he wanted to customize it, the man refused to sell. After Walker explained that he wanted to make a copy of the famous 1951 Hirohata Mercury custom originally designed and crafted by George and Sam Barris of Los Angeles, the owner gave in.

The Hirohata Merc is a legendary custom car, and it's not surprising that Walker wanted to make a clone. Bob Hirohata took his 1951 Mercury to the Barris brothers for a complete customization. Finished in time for the 1952 Motorama auto show, it was a sensation that put the Barris brothers on the map.

Walker commissioned Doug Thompson, then of Raytown but now of Butler, Mo., to replicate the famous Barris Merc. "He could do anything with his hands," Walker said. Thompson and Walker built the car by looking at photos of the original, which had been lost for years. Walker's car was finished in July of 1985, and he hauled it to a show in Springfield, Ohio. As he rolled it off the trailer, it drew such a crowd that he realized he and Thompson had created something very special.

"I built it to drive," Walker said, but it has changed his life in ways he could have never imagined. He said that taking the car to shows all across the country enabled him to meet people and do all kinds of things. Photos of the car have appeared in 200 magazines around the world. He has become friends with George Barris and some of his workmen who created the original.

The seafoam green two-door is long and low. It hugs the road and always looks like it is in motion. It defines an era when body men chopped tops, lengthened fenders and grafted parts of one car onto another, creating a completely new car out of the original. Using welding torches, body hammers and ingots of lead, these artists in welding helmets created rolling sculptures that are still unique. Many of the original cars have been lost or destroyed, which is why guys like Walker want to re-create them. Walker also owns another Barris replica called Blue Danube.

Jack Walker is crazy about custom cars from the 1950s. He commisioned a copy of the famous George Barris Hirohata Mercury. The Hirohata Merc is so popular that a model has been made of it.

Years after Walker's car was finished, the original Hirohata Merc was found. Through the efforts of many people, a 10-year restoration brought it back to life. Jim McNeill of California owns it. Walker says with a grin that his car is closer to the original than the restoration is.

What will he do with his beloved Mercury? "I'll never sell it," he said. But eventually he will probably donate it to Darryl Starbird's National Rod & Custom Car Hall of Fame Museum in Afton, Okla., so it can live out the rest of its life being seen by the public instead of languishing in obscurity.

Artwork is best when it's appreciated, and there's no question that custom cars of this caliber are artwork.

'38 Ford

Ryan Cochran preaches the hot rod gospel

Ryan Cochran is young, but he lives in the past, at least in terms of his automotive interests. He's fascinated with old-school hot rods, the kind that you would have seen in 1950.

Cochran has an everyday job in the Internet technology world, but when it comes to cars, he and his Kansas City friend Kevin Lee are steeped in tradition.

Cochran, formerly of Kansas City and now of

Austin, Texas, hosts a cool Web site called jalopy-journal.com. Its message board is a lifeline for hot rodders from all across the country, and it spreads the hot rod gospel from coast to coast and beyond.

On his Web site, Cochran writes: "The Jalopy Journal was formed… to spread the gospel of traditional Hot Rods and Kustoms to hoodlums worldwide... We wanted to be the voice of the working man, a tool in the toolbox of the guy that does it himself, and a place where citizen journalists could show the "big-time" media a thing or two. We haven't done it all yet, but we aim to in time...

Traditional hot rods are experiencing a

resurgence, and Lee and Cochran are riding the crest of a new wave.

Cochran's car is a pristine 1938 Ford coupe that he drives at least once a week. Because its fenders have a few rock chips, he said his '38 is too rough to be perfect, yet it's still too nice to be a rat rod. Cochran found the body in a barn. It still has its original black paint, although it has been polished and coated with clear lacquer. It now sits on a modified aftermarket frame. The Mustang II front suspension has airbags for ground clearance while driving. The rear axle has coil-over shocks.

There's nothing old school about the engine, a

Ryan Cochran's interest in hot rods and custom cars has become a vocation. His Jalopy Journal is his online publication. Right: Kevin Lee of Kansas City built a traditional hot rod roadster.

Cochran's 1938 Ford coupe looks pretty conservative, but a 600-horsepower Chevrolet racing engine sits under the hood.

424-cubic-inch Chevrolet race engine that has been de-tuned for the street. Cochran surmises that it pumps more than 600 horsepower through a four-speed transmission into a 9-inch rear axle.

Lee's hot rod is about as traditional as a car can be. It looks exactly like something from 1950. The chopped roadster body sits on a Model A frame. It has a flathead Ford engine that Lee found in a junk store. He made the streamlined nose from commercial trash-can lids.

Handmade, spun-aluminum wheel covers fit over wire wheels that are mounted with skinny reproduction tires. The gas tank is bolted above the rear axle.

Lee's rod is pure nostalgia. It represents a time when a hot rod was experimental, dirty and more about innovation than money. The crude paint, hand lettering and bare interior capture that essence. ∎

Dreams of Desire

Chapter Five

The ornery cackle of our Volkswagen GTI's exhaust floated through the open bedroom window as I lay reading in bed. I listened as son Jon scurried out of the drive and headed to a friend's house.

Ten minutes later the garage door opened, but I didn't hear his car.

"Oh no," I thought, and instinctively began to get out of bed.

"Dad . . .?" The plaintive wail of my son's trembling voice chilled me like ice. He had run five blocks home, and he was out of breath.

"Dad, a strange car followed me, and I cut through the parking lot behind the church. I hit a curb."

Our little GTI, the one I bought new, then sold, then bought again years later, was wrecked.

I threw on some clothes and went to check out the damage. As we drove, the silence was palpable; my rage seethed just under the surface. Jon fidgeted.

The GTI sat crumpled in the dark, listing to one side. The small beam of my flashlight showed the wheel and tire jammed up under the fender. The damage was far worse than a broken wheel.

I was so angry I could hardly talk. I wanted to scream about carelessness, and trying to ditch the "strange car," but I knew I would erupt if I said anything.

As I paced and fumed, I began to calm down. We were fortunate no one had been hurt. And it was just a car, after all.

Why was this nine-year-old car so dear to me? When I bought it in 1984, it was my personal pet. I reveled in every minute behind the wheel.

A couple of years later, the GTI was replaced by a Porsche 944. The woman who bought the GTI loved it as much as I did, and she called occasionally to let me know how it was doing.

Six years later, she called to say the GTI was for sale. I couldn't resist her invitation to take it for one last drive. Imagine how shocked I was to find it like the day I sold it. No dents, no scratches and only 51,000 miles. When I fired it up, all of the old sensations flooded back. The exhaust still popped and cracked with each shift. I ran my fingers over the radio, which I had installed in my garage. It felt as if someone had turned the clock back nine years.

A couple of days later, the GTI was back in our garage. My 16-year-old son had just gotten his driver's license and we could have used another car. Besides, I liked the idea of rekindling our romance. Little did I know how that GTI would teach me such an important lesson.

My son Jon's words, written when he was the editor of the high school newspaper, say it better than I ever could:

"In 1984, my dad fulfilled a dream. He bought a brand-new, white Volkswagen Rabbit GTI. He cleaned and cared for it with the caution of a mother tending a newborn child. It was his baby. Nine years later, and two or three cars later, I had been entrusted with the keys of his firstborn.

"Just keeping the car up to his standards was a challenge all in itself. I can't count the number of times he asked me if I thought that car was my own personal trash can. Of course, I always thought it was immaculate.

"These small altercations I could handle, but there was one occurrence that I couldn't. As I drove through a parking lot in the dark of night something happened that changed my life. My car came over the crown of a small hill, and the lights focused on a median. I hit the brakes. It was too late; the axle was bent and the frame pushed back.

" After arriving at the scene, my dad stood isolated in the parking lot with flames in his eyes. I was going to be disowned. After minutes that seemed hours, my dad came back to his car to go home. His devilish eyes suddenly had an ethereal coolness. His arm found its way around my shoulder. There was no doubt that he was upset, but his words and actions brought comfort. It proved to me that perhaps I am his baby." ■

— Tom Strongman

California Gleamin'

To the automotive faithful, nothing can surpass the annual Pebble Beach Concours d'Elegance

The 18th fairway of the Pebble Beach Golf Links is one of the most storied holes in golf. Tom Watson curled in a 20-foot putt to take the 1982 U.S. Open from Jack Nicklaus after chipping in a sensational birdie on 17.

On the third Sunday of August, however, the 18th fairway witnesses legendary drives of a different sort. More than 200 of the finest automobiles roll onto the manicured grass for the Pebble Beach Concours d'Elegance. It's hard to imagine a setting more vivid.

For 56 years, the auto faithful have made Pebble Beach an annual pilgrimage. Die-hard aficionados arrive by 6 a.m. to place blankets near the presentation ramp, securing a ringside seat for trophy

This stunning Talbot-Lago coupe, designed by French coachbuilder Figoni et Falaschi, is owned by the Nethercutt Collection. The 1947 Rolls-Royce Silver Wraith Inskip Cabriolet, upper right, speaks elegance.

presentations later in the afternoon.

There's something magical about being there before sunrise when show cars slip through the chill and half-light of dawn to find their parking spots. One minute the straight-pipe exhaust of a Delahaye Grand Prix car splits the early-morning fog, while the next minute a Rolls-Royce whispers past so quietly it seems like an apparition.

Pebble Beach is a visual feast. It is ladies in picture-book hats, Mimosas at 10 a.m. and picnic lunches spread beside priceless automobiles. Stroll the lawn for a couple of hours, and your senses are overwhelmed. Exceptional cars are so plentiful that the spectacular becomes commonplace.

The Pebble Beach concours is the highlight of a four-day automotive celebration on the Monterey peninsula that also includes Concorso Italiano, The Quail - A Motorsports Gathering, and the Monterey Historic Automobile Races at nearby Laguna Seca racetrack. ■

Upper left: The 1951 Talbot-Lago Grand Sport Saoutchik Coupe is one of a kind. Above: Sam and Emily Mann's 1937 Delage D8-120 S Pourtout Aero Coupe won Best of Show in 2005. Left: High heels and dress clothes don't stop owners from last-minute cleaning.

'39 Packard

Jack and Lois Barton cherish their Cantrell-bodied woodie

Jack Barton's 1939 Packard Six station wagon with its Cantrell body takes your breath away. It is as much a piece of fine furniture as it is an automobile, and Barton's restoration is absolutely perfect.

J.T. Cantrell of Huntington, N.Y., was a well-known maker of woodie station wagons. He built wagons for a variety of brands, but converted only 25 Packards in 1939. Only five are known to exist today, and Barton's car is one.

Barton, of Gallatin, Mo., runs a hardware business and collects old cars. He began searching for a woodie in 1995 after attending the Antique Automobile Club of America's annual meeting in Hershey, Pa. He asked his wife, Lois, and daughters, Sara and Anna, which cars they liked best. "The woodies," they answered. The search was on.

He located this unrestored car in Florida. It was basically complete but needed a total restoration.

The Packard has a 245-cubic-inch, six-cylinder engine and an overdrive transmission. It cost $1,404 new. It weighs 3,600 pounds and has a 122-inch wheelbase.

Barton took more than 1,000 photos as he carefully dismantled the car. He removed the wood body and shipped it to John David Hamlin in Indiana. Hamlin had woodworking experience but had never undertaken a project like this. He replicated every piece of wood in Honduran mahogany or maple. His workmanship is astounding.

While Hamlin took a couple of years to fabri-

Jack and Lois Barton are justifiably proud of their Packard. The wood body is finished as nicely as fine furniture, and the attention to detail is outstanding.

cate the wood body, Barton disassembled, restored and reassembled the rest of the car. It is like new, top and bottom, inside and out. Even the radiator hose clamps are original. The engine is cleaner than most kitchens. Kevin Zwygart,

Cowgill, Mo., did the paint and bodywork. Garry Westher of Richmond, Mo., helped Barton with the reassembly.

"We built it to drive, but finished it to show," Barton said. And show it does.

The Packard has garnered numerous Best of Show accolades. One of its most revered is the 2004 People's Choice award from Wavecrest, a gathering of more than 300 woodies in Encinitas, Calif. ■

Racine

Dan Root created a vision by hand

Dan Root's philosophy of car building is simple. "If you're willing to build a car one-eighth of an inch at a time," it's amazing what can be accomplished.

Root has been tinkering with cars and hot rods since the 1950s. The inspiration for this car, which he calls Racine because it is the French word for "root," came when he was working on a 1933 Ford roadster. "Every night, when I would go into the house (from the garage), I would look back at the fender slope of my '33 and think, 'Man, if I could just build that car and put a lower body on it.'"

From that simple dream, thoughts of Racine began to take shape in his mind. Root decided to create a roadster with swooping lines that recalled cars created by legendary 1930s European coach builders such as Figoni and Falaschi, Delahaye and Talbot. In those cars he saw a visual connection to some traditional hot rod shapes and he set about translating his dream into metal.

The first welding spark that kindled Racine was struck more than five years ago. Construction started with the cockpit, cowl, doors and trunk of an MG-B, which Root mounted atop a 1934 Ford frame. He extended the wheelbase 20 inches, putting the extra length in front. He added 1934 Ford front fenders and running boards, a 1938 Ford hood and the upper half of a 1938 Ford grille. The rear fenders came from a 1936 Ford, but Root patiently extended them 10 inches to give the car a longer, lower look. Headlights are from a 1937 Plymouth, the turn signals are from a Harley-Davidson, and the taillights are from a 1938 Oldsmobile.

For power, Root fitted a 3.4-liter V-6 modified by Anderson Racing. The transmission is a T-5 aluminum five-speed manual. The rear suspension has leaf springs and racing shock absorbers, while the front suspension is a modified racing design.

Root's long-fendered, curvaceous roadster

Dan Root created his car by melding pieces of many cars. The cockpit is from an MG-B, the fenders are from a '34 Ford and the grille is a from a '38 Ford.

turned out so well that even seasoned car fanatics can't tell what it is. It's the kind of car you would expect to see in a Clark Gable movie. Street rodders turn a blind eye to it, but the sports-car set loves it. It has been displayed at the Arthritis Foundation's annual Concours d'Elegance.

Root says Racine is probably his last big project. But then he begins talking about replicating an open-wheel Mercedes-Benz from the 1930s, and there's a Studebaker coupe in storage, and, well, you get the picture. Car guys who love to be creative can't stop the juices from flowing. "You might as well be out in the garage welding on a car," he said with a laugh.

'50 Silver Wraith

This Rolls-Royce goes from derelict to prizewinner

Elliot Kaplan, left, and Jim Daniels transformed this Rolls-Royce into a showpiece. It was honored with Best of Show and the Hooper Award by the Rolls-Royce Owner's Club. It also won a Blue Ribbon and the People's Choice at the Meadow Brook Concours d'Elegance.

The Hooper-bodied 1950 Rolls-Royce Silver Wraith has a Cinderella quality to it. This elegant limousine, owned by Elliot M. Kaplan of Stilwell and James F. B. Daniels of Kansas City, went from a used-car dealer on Independence Avenue to winning Best of Show at the Rolls-Royce Owner's Club national meet in Pebble Beach, Calif.

Daniels spotted this significant vehicle about six years ago. The aluminum body was dented and unkempt after years of neglect, but the odometer read only 12,000 miles. Daniels and his law partner Kaplan bought the car together. Little did they know it was a very special Rolls.

Kaplan and Daniels discovered that this car was originally built for Lord Kemsley, a publishing magnate who owned the *London Daily Telegraph*, *Sunday Times* and *Financial Times*. The body is a one-off design by Hooper and Co., coachbuilders to the royal family. Rolls-Royce bought the car back from Lord Kemsley and used it to chauffeur dignitaries. The car still has the original Rolls-Royce factory license plates.

A San Francisco stockbroker brought the Rolls to this country in 1961. It's not clear exactly when it came to Kansas City, but Kaplan thinks the Hall family bought it to chauffeur prospective clients around developments in Johnson County.

After buying the car, Kaplan and Daniels sent it to Ralph Curzon of Hyphen Repair in Toronto. Curzon was trained at the Rolls-Royce factory, and he began the laborious process of restoring this special car to its original glory. The hand-formed body is unique. Its frame is English Ash with bronze reinforcements.

Curzon's work is stunning. As beautiful as the body is, the undercarriage looks exactly as it did the day the car was new. All of the bolts are cadmium plated, for example, and their square heads are perfectly aligned.

The frame glistens, and the running gear is spotless. The rear springs are sheathed in leather and automatically lubricated.

The six-cylinder engine is as quiet as it is smooth, and it idles like a sewing machine.

The Silver Wraith's interior is warm and inviting. Matching walnut is used throughout the interior, which has wool seats and deep pile carpeting in back.

Getting the car ready for the national show was like getting Cinderella ready for the ball. A month before the car was transported to Pebble Beach, the left front fender was damaged slightly. The fender was removed and sent to Canada for repair. Bill Durham of the First Team Carstar Collision body shop in Stilwell hurriedly repainted it.

The night before the car was to leave, the clock ceased working. Sham Agayev of Tivol Jewels fabricated parts and cleaned the clock over night so the car could leave on schedule. The payoff for all this last-minute work was not only the Best in Show trophy but also the Hooper Award. The glass slipper was a perfect fit. ■

Ralph Curzon's restoration is superb. Every nut and bolt on the chassis is like new. The interior is as cozy as an English drawing room and just as quiet.

'55 Ford Thunderbird

Ron Portland and his Thunderbird have grown up together

When Ron Portland drove his car to Parsons College, he rented a house with a garage. After college, he stored the car in his family's garage for 30 years. He had it repainted about 10 years ago.

Ron Portland's interest in cars has its roots in a very special 1955 Ford Thunderbird. They first met in 1954, and he has owned it for more than 40 years.

Portland, now of Kansas City, was born in Dearborn, Mich., home of Ford Motor Co. Dearborn was home to many Ford managers, and Portland's family knew many of them as neighbors. One was Robert S. McNamara, one of the famous Ford "Whiz Kids" and later secretary of defense in the Kennedy and Johnson administrations.

Portland first saw a Thunderbird in November of 1954. His family had moved to Philadelphia, and a Ford executive, driving a black Thunderbird, stopped by their house. He gave young Portland a ride. In later years, Portland's dad insisted the visiting Ford executive was Lee Iacocca, although Portland can't prove that. "I can't be positive, and Dad's no longer with us, but he probably wouldn't change his story," Portland said with a smile.

In 1965, Portland's mom bought him a 1955 Thunderbird, and he's quite sure it is the very same car he rode in. The car's data plate indicates that it was one of the first 1,000, and it was built in October of 1954.

When Portland went to Parsons College in Fairfield, Iowa, the Thunderbird went, too. He rented a house so he could have a garage for his black beauty. It survived his college days without serious incident.

After college, Portland moved to Chicago and then to New York city. New York was no place for a

October 1967

car, so he drove the T-Bird to Charlotte, N.C., and stored it in his parents' garage. It sat in storage for the next 30 years.

Portland's car is amazingly original. It has 76,000 miles. He had it painted 10 years ago and the seats re-covered.

Portland brought his car to Kansas City in 1999 shortly after he moved here. A couple of photographs of it are in Alan Tast's book *Thunderbird Fifty Years*. Tast lives in Olathe.

Portland and his mother, Isabel, now 89 years old and still driving, share a Thunderbird connection that goes beyond her buying this car for him when he was a youth. A couple of years ago she decided it would be fun to have one of the new-generation Thunderbirds. She owns a 2002. ■

'32 Packard Deluxe Eight

Jon Root started liking Packards when he was two years old

Jon and Bonney Root bought their Packard to drive, and they love cruising through their neighborhood on warm summer evenings. Friends often ride in the rumble seat.

Jon Root of Leawood has loved Packards since he took his first drive in one at age 2. That's right. Drive, not ride.

Root's eyes twinkle as he tells the story. Root's father passed away in 1940 when Root was 2. After that, he and his mom were often visited by two family friends who owned Packard convertible coupes, one a 1930 and one 1932. Root used to love riding in the rumble seat as they went on errands. One day while the adults were visiting, Root climbed into the Packard and accidentally bumped it out of gear. It rolled slowly down the drive backward, but a passing paperboy jumped in and put on the brake. Root laughs when he says he thinks he was the youngest person to ever drive a Packard.

The images of those early Packards left an indelible impression on Root. He loved the huge headlights, the big chrome stone guards in front of the radiator and the bright red hexagon emblems on the wire wheels. He always said he would have a Packard someday.

At age 63, he finally got the Packard he had wanted all his life. His car, which he calls the Green Queen, is a 1932 Deluxe Eight, model 903, style 519 and car No. 150. There are only 10 cars like it registered in the national Packard Club. This car originally cost $3,750, which was eight times more expensive than a 1932 Ford.

Root and his wife, Bonney, have had the Green Queen for five years. Root bought it from a dealer in Seattle. He knew from the moment he saw it

that he was going to buy it. Once he got it home and began to drive it, it was plagued by a periodic backfire. With help from Wilbur Haupt, a fellow Packard enthusiast, he checked the ignition system and fuel system but couldn't find the problem. His patience was wearing thin, and he began to think his car was never going to be right. One day, as he was looking around the gas tank with a flashlight, he discovered a twisted copper fuel line on top of the gas tank. He replaced the fitting, and now the car runs perfectly. The eight-cylinder engine is so quiet you can hardly hear it idle and the ride is magic-carpet smooth.

Jon and Bonney love to cruise in their Packard. They take it out three or four nights a week just to amble down quiet streets. But they have also driven it to Jamesport, Mo., and Wichita.

After 61 years of dreaming, Root has a Packard at last. The longer a dream stays alive, the sweeter it is once it's fulfilled. ∎

A special compartment for golf clubs opens just behind the passenger-side door. This Packard is a picture of elegance.

'36 Chevy

Rich Rowe's Chevy reminds him of early days with his brother

Rich Rowe named his car after his brother because they used to drive around Pennsylvania when Rich was 10 years old.

I t's not unusual for a car to have a nickname, and Rich Rowe lovingly named his 1936 Chevrolet "Dave," after his deceased older brother.

Rowe, of Edgerton, Kan., said that his twin older brothers, John and Dave, bought a '36 Chevy and cruised it around the coal region of Shamokin, Pa., when he was about 10 years old. John enlisted in the Army, but Dave was rejected because of a congenital heart condition. Dave and Rowe were buddies while John was in the service.

Dave insisted that Rowe, at age 12, learn to drive the Chevy, ostensibly so he could take his brother Dave to the hospital in case he "had the big one."

"We pulled the seat all the way forward, added a cushion from an old green couch and a pair of pillows for a back rest," he wrote in an article for the newsletter of the Vintage Chevrolet Club of America. "I could see over the hood and reach the floorboard pedals. I was driving."

In the ensuing years, Rowe's brother owned a

succession of cars, but Rowe always liked the '36 best. Dave died in 1962.

Rowe found another 1936 Chevrolet Master Deluxe in 1974 when his brother-in-law moved to Valley City, N.D., but it wasn't for sale. A couple of years later, after the Chevy had been sitting in a field where it became a home for mice and rust, Rowe was finally able to buy it.

Rowe got rid of the mice, fired it up and took his wife, Anne, for a ride. "We did a few doughnuts," he wrote.

When Rowe moved to Edgerton in 1990, he left the Chevy in North Dakota to be restored. For five years it was neglected as the restoration shop shuffled between owners. Rowe rescued it once again and this time vowed to keep it. That's when he named it "Dave."

Mike Doll of Northland Auto Restoration in Mandan, N.D., restored the '36, and Rowe took it to Edgerton.

"I know my brother Dave is out there somewhere," Rowe said, "grinning from ear to ear." ■

It took many years for Rowe to get his Chevy restored, but the final result is outstanding. Rowe says his brother Dave is "out there somewhere, grinning ear to ear."

'29 Rolls-Royce

Roger Morrison's stunning Springfield Phantom I Riviera

Roger Morrison has been intrigued by the Rolls-Royce since he was a child. He now has several in his collection, and this Riviera is one of his favorites.

Roger Morrison's first two words were "car" and "truck." His fascination with cars started at an early age.

As a youngster, he would lie in bed on a summer night with the window open. As cars passed, he tried to identify the brand by the sound of the engine. At the last second, he would pop up and look out the window to see whether his guess was right.

Morrison's car hobby has blossomed into an eclectic collection of wonderful vehicles. It all stemmed, he said, from a 1960 *Road & Track* magazine article about a Rolls-Royce Silver Cloud II.

"I sat here in Salina, Kansas, and wondered if I could ever ride in one. My ultimate dream would be to own one," he said. Today that dream has wheels, and he and his wife, Sissy, own a 1929 Rolls-Royce Springfield Phantom I Riviera Town Brougham with a body by Brewster. The Riviera's coach-built body was placed on a chassis built in Rolls-Royce's Springfield, Mass., factory. The factory was in existence from 1921 to 1931.

The rear half of Morrison's Riviera looks like a horse-drawn carriage, while the long hood and sweeping fenders convey power and speed. This magnificent vehicle was the pinnacle of the Roarin' 20s, and it was delivered to Mrs. Irene M. Carman of New York City on Dec. 12, 1929. Trimmed with gold and inlaid with delicate wood, it cost well over $20,000. That price is equivalent to more than $236,000 in today's dollars.

The Riviera survived the Depression and World War II intact, as its owners resisted the temptation to send it back to the factory or sell it for scrap. Morrison bought the car from a friend about eight years ago.

Rick Hamlin of Rick's Auto Restoration in Wellington, Kan., completed a stunning restoration. One thing he carefully preserved is the hand-painted canework on the rear of the body. The faux caning is an art carried over from carriage days. It took two to three months for an artisan to apply the horizontal, then vertical and then diagonal lines by squeezing thickened paint through a funnel, much as a pastry chef decorates a cake. The caning is in remarkable condition given its age.

Hamlin's restoration has resulted in numerous awards. The Riviera was judged first in its class and awarded the J.B. Nethercutt trophy for Most Elegant Closed Car at the 2003 Pebble Beach Concours d'Elegance. In 2004 it was named Most Outstanding Rolls-Royce at the 2004 Amelia Island Concours.

The rear seat of the Rolls-Royce is as cozy as a palace on wheels. Ladies' perfume bottles are built into the right-hand door.

'32 Ford

Roger Morrison approaches his hot rod hobby as if he were an automotive archaeologist.

He loves digging up old cars, tracking down their history and putting them back to original condition.

One of his treasures is the black and white, 1932 Ford originally built by Pat and Tony Berardini. The brothers raced their roadster on drag strips near Los Angeles, and it won 80 percent of its races in six years. They were champions from 1950 to 1955.

The engine is a 314-cubic-inch Ford flathead with Harrell finned aluminum heads, four carburetors and an Iskenderian 404 camshaft. The Berardini Brothers' success with the Isky 404 cam is why the car is called 404 Jr.

The brothers sold the car in 1955, and,it passed through two more owners before Morrison saw it in 2004 at the Grand National Roadster Show. Morrison bought the car from Rudy Perez, its third owner, and sent it to Dave Crouse, owner of Custom Auto in Loveland, Colo. Crouse studied old photos and consulted with Pat Berardini as he restored 404 Jr. Alan Johnson replicated Von Dutch's original pinstriping.

Morrison delights in locating historically significant hot rods and having Crouse restore them. It seems redundant to say that automotive history is about the cars, but so often, historically significant cars get modified, trashed or destroyed, and that's especially true with hot rods. Because of the foresight of collectors such as Morrison, many classic hot rods are being rescued and restored. ∎

The Berardini Brothers' racer was exceptionally successful in its six years on a track. The seats were pirated from a bomber.

The Smith Collection

Bill Smith's engine museum is a cathedral of speed

Bill Smith started collecting engine parts when he was 16 years old. That collection has evolved into a museum that contains more than 600 engines, including many rare racing engines. A garage scene, right, depicts an old racer's hangout.

B ill Smith's museum in Lincoln, Neb., is a monument to the genius of men who racked their brains and dirtied their fingernails to find a faster way to the finish line. Smith's collection of more than 600 engines is a three-dimensional history book, and strolling through the three-story structure is like walking on hallowed ground. The presence of men such as Harry Miller, Leo Goossen and Fred Offenhauser, to name three, is almost palpable.

The three-story Smith Collection sits next to Smith's Speedway Motors.

"Speedy" Bill and Joyce Smith founded the company in 1952. Known as "America's Oldest Speed Shop," Speedway Motors is an enterprise that manufactures and sells, through catalogs and the Internet, more than 8,000 products for racers and hotrod enthusiasts. The company employs 162 people at a building complex that occupies 520,000 square feet on 42 acres just west of downtown Lincoln.

Smith started collecting engine parts when he was 16 years old because he was fascinated with the ingenuity of guys who were trying to find a better way to make a car go faster. Each engine in Smith's museum has been meticulously polished, painted and prepared to look better than it ever

did when new. Many are overrestored to attract attention and interest. "We're just like a funeral home," he said. "When you went to see your uncle, granddad or whomever in the funeral home, he probably looked nicer than he had looked in a long, long time. He had a little rouge on his cheeks, the tobacco juice was off his teeth and his clothes were clean. We make engines look as nice as we can."

Smith always had a special admiration for Harry Miller. A special room just inside the museum's front door contains seven of Miller's designs plus

Leo Goossen's drafting table.

The Miller room is like a chapel in Smith's cathedral of speed. Each engine is displayed like fine artwork.

"The world has acknowledged that Harry Miller is the true father of speed," Smith said. "Not just American speed, but the world."

"Speedy" Bill raced motorcycles, and then road-sters, on the dirt tracks of Nebraska in 1949. He quickly realized that it was better to be an owner, builder and designer than a driver, and thus began a long history of success. In the 1950s and 1960s, Smith raced dragsters, stock cars, NASCAR, Bonneville, Indy, modifieds and sprint cars.

In the 1970s he raced Champ dirt cars and sprint cars with drivers who were the original "Outlaws." He won the Sprint Car Nationals and the Hulman 100. Driving legends such as Jan Opperman, Doug Wolfgang, Tiny Lund, Larry Dickson and Ron Shuman piloted Smith's cars.

In addition to engines, the Smith Collection also houses 74 vehicles, including a Tucker and a 1935 Ford Indy car.

Smith's long involvement in racing, especially the Indianapolis 500, inspired him to re-create a section of the Indianapolis Motor Speedway's historic Gasoline Alley complete with two original garage doors.

Smith is a model of low-key, Midwestern manners. He is hardly ever without his trademark High Roller hat, one he started wearing in the 1970s so people would remember him. He still puts in 10-hour days and credits his wife, Joyce, who serves as the company's corporate secretary-treasurer, as an integral part of his success. Sons

Carson, Craig, Clay and Jason also work in the company.

One of Smith's favorite sayings is: "I never sold anybody anything they ever needed. I have nothing that extends their life. I'm selling things that make them feel good and help fulfill their dreams."

Gazing across his collection, Smith says, "Almost everything I look at I was either involved in it, or knew the guy who was doing it or had some kind of a touch-feel relationship with it. I have so many one-offs that you couldn't replicate what you see here even if you had all of your friends in the world trying to help you do it."

The Smith Collection is more than a repository for some of the most individual, creative and unique engines ever conceived. It is a house of dreams, a living catalog that chronicles racing almost since racing began. But most of all, the Smith Collection is a testimony to Bill and Joyce Smith's dedication, hard work and the ability to make their dream come true. ∎

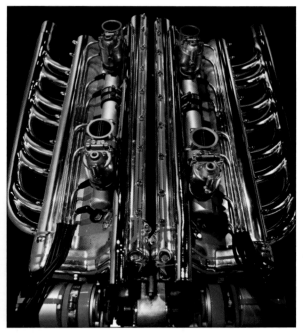

Smith's museum has a special room to showcase engines designed by Harry Miller. Miller's midget engine, opposite page, looks like a pipe organ. The 16-cylinder, above, is a jewel. Left: A Hisso engine looks especially intimidating because of its finned exhaust pipe.

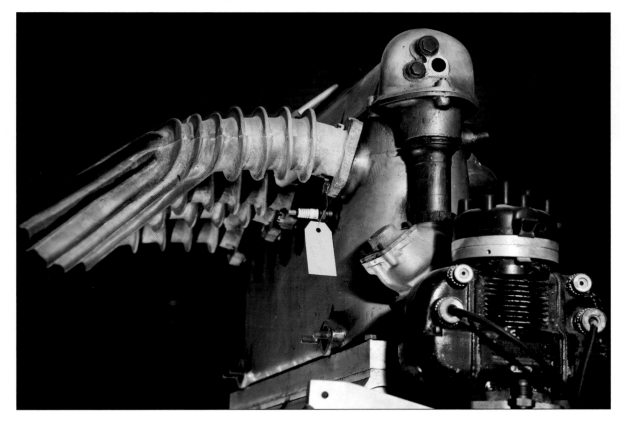

Tomorrow's classics?

Will today's cars become future collectibles

Many of today's exotic automobiles are works of art. The simple geometry of a Porsche Carerra GT, right, or the headlight of a Pontiac Solstice, above, has a lot of eye appeal.

There's little doubt that vintage cars can be works of art. Who can turn away from the soaring beauty of a perfectly restored 1939 Packard with a Cantrell wood body, or how about the swoop and swirl of the sheet metal draped across a Hooper-bodied 1950 Rolls-Royce Silver Wraith?

Today's cars represent a truly golden era of motoring. Look around the Greater Kansas City International Auto Show and you'll see hundreds of vehicles that vie for your attention. Electronic engine controls and supercomputers enable engineers and designers to create vehicles that would have been unheard of just two decades ago. High-horsepower, low-emission engines are commonplace, and space-age technology lets companies build cars that are lighter, and stronger, than ever before. Aluminum bodies, high-tech composites and aluminum frames can be found on sports and luxury cars.

Sophisticated speedsters such as the Porsche Carrera GT or the Mercedes-Benz McLaren SLR reach for the pinnacle of both design and performance. Hybrids, by combining gasoline engines and electric motors, are more efficient with each new generation.

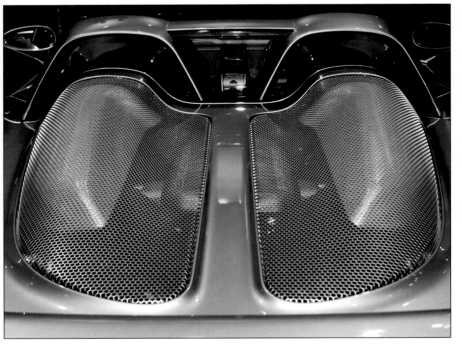

The cars of tomorrow may have bodies made of plastic and propulsion systems such as hydrogen or a fuel cell, but whatever, cars will continue to excite and titillate. In the end, what makes any car special is not just its style or performance, but its place in the fabric of our lives and the memories that it carries. ■

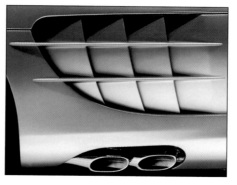

New cars can be four-wheeled sculpture. Check out the detailing on the Mercedes-Benz McLaren SLR, above. An Acura concept coupe, below, shows flashes of brilliance in the subtle surfaces of its body.